ADVANCE PRAISE

"The evolution of financial science has improved the lives of real people, and Josh Itzoe has helped to channel this spirit by advocating for evidence-based investing in retirement accounts. His contributions continue in his new book, The Fiduciary Formula, a comprehensive guide that will help fiduciaries in their quest to continuously improve outcomes for 401(k) plan participants."

—DAVID BOOTH, FOUNDER AND EXECUTIVE
CHAIRMAN OF DIMENSIONAL FUND ADVISORS LP

"I have admired Josh for many years. He is a pioneer in our industry, and at the forefront of helping retirement plan fiduciaries understand their responsibilities and navigate the complexities of ERISA. Anyone serving as a retirement plan fiduciary would be well served by reading this book. Your company, your participants, and your fellow committee members will be happy you did."

—FIELDING MILLER, CEO AND CO-FOUNDER OF CAPTRUST

"The Fiduciary Formula is an insightful and timely book that provides practical guidance for overseeing and managing a retirement plan in a changing world. If you are a fiduciary, read this book! It will help you make sound decisions for your organization and your employees."

—ANN SCHLECK, PRINCIPAL AT INSPIREDMEETINGS BY
ANN SCHLECK AND FORMER NATIONAL PRACTICE LEADER
FOR DEFINED CONTRIBUTION PLANS AT DELOITTE

"A 'fiduciary' (fi*du*ci*ar*y) is a person or institution that has the power to act on behalf of another in situations that require the utmost trust, honesty, and loyalty. They are legally bound to provide the 'highest standard of care.' They must always act in the beneficiary's best interest, even if doing so is contrary to their own. For a financial advisor, this may mean recommending a product that results in reduced or no compensation because it is the best option for the client.

"However, in the financial services industry, the distinction between fiduciary advice and 'product distributor' is neither recognized nor understood by the public. It's unfortunate, but true, that people do not know how to identify financial advice that is truly in their best interest. More than half of investors believe their advisor is operating much like their accountant, attorney, or doctor, and falsely believe all advisors are legally required to always act in their clients' best interests. That means these obligations extend beyond the first meeting. A fiduciary will continually monitor a client's investments and financial situation and adhere to best practices of conduct for the duration of the relationship.

"Josh Itzoe has been an Accredited Investment Fiduciary® (AIF®) Designee since 2007. He mastered the four-step process detailed in his AIF® Designation training and through his work he embodies fiduciary excellence: organizing clients' portfolios for success, formalizing an investment strategy, conducting due diligence and implementing the strategy, and monitoring fees, results and providers.

"The Fiduciary Formula is brilliant because it is elegant in its simplicity and is easy to understand and implement. Josh is correct, there is no perfect corporate retirement plan but by using The Fiduciary Formula, you can optimize your plan for successful outcomes."

—MATTHEW WOLNIEWICZ, PRESIDENT OF FI360

"Josh Itzoe has crafted an easily digested guide that corporate leaders would be wise to read. They can thank him later when they avoid the risk, expense, and headaches that other plan sponsors will sadly endure. I especially enjoyed Josh's explanation of the conflicts of interest that are sometimes hard to see."

—GREG LONG, FORMER MANAGING FIDUCIARY OF THE U.S. GOVERNMENT'S THRIFT SAVINGS PLAN

THE FIDUCIARY FORMULA

THE
Fiduciary
Formula

6 ESSENTIAL ELEMENTS to Create
the Perfect Corporate Retirement Plan

JOSH ITZOE

LIONCREST

PUBLISHING

THE FIDUCIARY FORMULA

6 Essential Elements to Create the Perfect Corporate Retirement Plan

ISBN   978-1-5445-1523-6   *Hardcover*

         978-1-5445-1522-9   *Paperback*

         978-1-5445-1521-2   *Ebook*

Contents

Disclaimer 11

Foreword 13

Introduction 17

1. My Story..21

2. The Fiduciary Formula..27

3. It All Starts with the Committee (Fg)...................................33

4. Developing and Equipping Your Committee (Fg) 37

5. Engaging Your Committee (Fg)..43

6. Behavioral Finance Concepts (Pd)..53

7. Focusing on Replacement Rates (Pd) 59

8. Adoption of Automatic Features (Pd) 63

9. Implementing an Automatic Features Strategy (Pd) 71

10. The Evolution of the Fee Landscape (Fs) 81

11. Litigation Trends (Fs) 87

12. Assessing the Risks (Fs) 93

13. Understanding Plan Economics (Fs)......................................101

14. Revenue Sharing and Conflicts of Interest (Fs) 109

15. Asset-Based versus Fixed Fees (Fs) 119

16. IPS Best Practices (Ip) 133

17. Emerging Trends in Fund Menu Design (Ip) 139

18. Target Date Fund Selection and Monitoring (Ip) 145

19. The Evidence for Passive Management (Ip)............................149

20. Putting Investment Theory into Practice (Ip)........................159

21. Financial Wellness versus Financial Well-Being (Ps) 167

22. Gender, Age, and Income Differences (Ps)............................173

23. Participant Strategies, Ideas, and Recommendations (Ps)...........177

24. Developing Strong Service Provider Partnerships (Pm)...........187

25. What to Look for in a Fiduciary Advisor (Pm)......................191

26. What to Look for in a Recordkeeper/TPA (Pm)....................197

27. What to Look for in a Plan Auditor (Pm)..............................209

28. The Fiduciary of the Future...223

Conclusion 241

Acknowledgments 243

About the Author..245

Notes..247

Index 253

Disclaimer

Josh Itzoe is a co-founder, partner, and chief strategy officer at Greenspring Advisors, a registered investment adviser (RIA). He is a CERTIFIED FINANCIAL PLANNER™ professional and Accredited Investment Fiduciary®. The information presented by the author and the publisher is for informational and educational purposes only. It should not be considered specific investment advice, does not take into consideration your specific situation, and does not intend to make an offer or solicitation for the sale or purchase of any securities or investment strategies. Additionally, no legal or tax advice is being offered. If legal or tax advice is needed, a qualified professional should be engaged. Investments involve risk and are not guaranteed. This book contains information that might be dated and is intended only to educate and entertain. Any links or websites referred to are for informational purposes only. Websites not associated with the author are unaffiliated sources of information, and the author takes no responsibility for the accuracy of the information provided by these websites. Be sure to consult with a qualified financial advisor, legal, and/or tax professional before implementing any strategy discussed herein.

Foreword

If you're reading this book, you're probably a decision-maker for a retirement plan (or someone who helps that person). In legal speak, the decision-makers for plans are called fiduciaries. But that's not just a name; instead, it's a doorway leading to a set of lengthy and complex rules. Courts have called those standards "the highest known to the law." In other words, the expectations placed on fiduciaries are very high.

To compound matters, you probably aren't a plan sponsor and a fiduciary because you set out to be one. Instead, your role as a business owner, manager, or executive puts you in the position of making decisions about a retirement plan—most likely a savings-based program, such as a 401(k) or 403(b) plan.

When you combine the fact that retirement plans aren't your primary business with "the highest standard known to the law," the potential downsides of doing it yourself are obvious. It seems like there are at least one or two new lawsuits every month against plan fiduciaries for breaching their duties. But that's not the mandated outcome; instead, it's a lesson that at least one person on your retirement plan team needs to be an expert (for example, an investment advisor whose practice focuses on retirement plans).

But even with help from an expert, fiduciaries still need to make plan decisions. And to make good decisions, fiduciaries need to understand the issues and the alternatives. That's not easy. Even the plan "language" can be confusing: QDIAs, TDFs, DIAs, 404(c), 404a-5, 408(b)(2). If you don't know what those acronyms or numbers mean, then you need information and advice to understand them and to comply with their requirements.

There are two messages in this discussion. First, get expert advice. Second, that's not enough. You also need to have a basic understanding of the language, the requirements, and the alternatives. That's what this book is about.

And while legal compliance is the foundation for doing your job as a retirement plan fiduciary, it's not the aspirational goal. That goal is to help your employees successfully save for a secure and confident retirement. That's not a legal requirement; it's a best practice. This book is also a primer on what you need to know to make decisions about best practices and how they can help your employees. Practices and successful plans also help plan sponsors by supporting a culture of loyalty and trust.

Fortunately, Josh Itzoe has the combination of qualities needed to write a book that matters. He is knowledgeable, a clear thinker, and a good writer. The complex concepts in retirement plans, the law, and investing are explained using the language of real people with real jobs. He avoids the industry jargon and the legal complexity, explaining what you need to understand in conversational language.

Josh also embraces best practices—both personally and professionally. As a result, he can, and does, walk the reader through the issues and decisions for developing a successful "best practices" retirement plan.

If you are going on a long journey with twisting and turning roads, you need a good roadmap. This book is the roadmap for your retirement plan journey, guiding you through the steps in the fiduciary and retirement plan journey. It starts with a foundation—a context—for understanding the journey and then moves on to:

- Fiduciary Governance (i.e., the internal structure you should have for managing your plan)
- Plan Design (i.e., how to design your plan for success)
- Fee Structure (i.e., how to avoid liability for the fees and costs that your plan pays)
- Investment Process (i.e., how to select and monitor your plan's investments for legal compliance and for best practices)
- Participant Support (i.e., how to embrace plan services to improve results for your employees)
- Provider Management (i.e., how to work with your plan's providers to achieve the best results)

This is an orderly and easy-to-understand approach. It also allows the reader to digest one subject at a time, which is helpful for an executive or manager with multiple demands on his or her time.

Fred Reish
Partner
Faegre Drinker

Introduction

WHO SHOULD READ THIS BOOK

I am more convinced than ever that the financial future of our country is built on the foundation of our existing retirement system. The financial success of every American worker covered by an ERISA (Employee Retirement Income Security Act) plan depends on our current generation of fiduciaries. They need us to exhibit courage, to exercise prudence and good judgment, and to fulfill our responsibilities as their representatives, protectors, and stewards.

My professional purpose is to make ERISA fiduciaries smarter. I strive to educate, coach, and inspire people in positions of decision-making authority to raise the bar. This book takes all that I've learned over the years as a successful retirement plan advisor and presents it in an introductory framework for members of the "fiduciary ecosystem."

The Fiduciary Formula is designed to be an actionable set of research-based ideas, best practices, and strategies that, when combined, creates better outcomes for everyone involved.

Let me define what I mean by the "fiduciary ecosystem." If you fall into one of these categories, this book is for you.

1. **Part-time fiduciaries**—These are named fiduciaries, plan trustees, and retirement plan committee members who have primary decision-making authority (known as "discretion" in ERISA) for the corporate retirement plan(s) at their organizations. They are rarely experts in retirement, investment, or fiduciary matters. They usually have little, if any, formalized training. Their primary job is not the retirement plan. Instead, they work in areas like finance, accounting, human resources, and operations. They are usually at an executive or management level (e.g., CFO, VP of HR, etc.).

2. **Full-time fiduciaries**—These are registered investment advisers or discretionary trustees, usually with a specialized focus on retirement plan consulting. They work with ERISA plans as a 3(21) and/or 3(38) fiduciary, either at the plan level and/or the participant level. They provide a broad range of services and deep fiduciary expertise to plan sponsors and participants.

3. **Part-time fiduciary support staff**—These are employees who support the part-time fiduciaries at their companies. They may work in accounting, payroll, or human resources. They are not formal committee members, and they don't have decision-making authority or discretion. They are responsible for implementing the decisions made by the fiduciaries. They help administer the retirement plan on a day-to-day basis and perform "ministerial" functions as defined by ERISA. This could be an HR generalist or benefits coordinator who provides enrollment materials or benefits information to new hires or submits enrollment forms to the plan's recordkeeper. It could also be a payroll specialist who remits contributions to the plan or processes deferral changes.

4. **Full-time fiduciary support staff**—These are industry pro-

fessionals and experts who range from recordkeepers to third-party administrators to plan auditors to ERISA and beyond. While the work these people do isn't considered fiduciary in nature, they are essential to the successful operation of a retirement plan, providing valuable support to both plan sponsors and participants.

There is no perfect corporate retirement plan. But there is a perfect corporate retirement plan for every company based on its unique goals, objectives, and resources. Using the Fiduciary Formula, I believe you will take steps to optimize your plan (or the plans you work with) for successful outcomes. It's also part of a broader platform of resources I created called Fiduciary U, which consists of a podcast, a blog, online courses, and other helpful resources. Visit FiduciaryU.com to learn more about and to download free tools and resources referenced throughout the book. Thanks for reading!

CHAPTER 1

My Story

I began working with 401(k) plans in late 2006, not long after we started Greenspring Advisors, a fee-only registered investment adviser (RIA). We structured the firm as a pure RIA with no broker-dealer affiliation and dropped all our securities licenses, allowing us to sell products and receive commissions or any other "indirect" compensation.

This was a rare business model in the industry at the time, but we gravitated to it for a very important reason—to work only on behalf of our clients with no compensation-related conflicts of interest. The prevailing model was to be a "fee-based" advisor, who could both charge clients fees and receive commissions on the sale of products, like stocks, mutual funds, annuities, and other insurance products. There were two problems with this approach. First, it created significant conflicts of interest, pitting the advisor and the client in an adversarial relationship. Second, these conflicts made it impossible to work only as a fiduciary to clients.

Let me share an example to illustrate the problem. Assume a client came to me with a $1 million portfolio they wanted me to invest for them. If I wasn't a fiduciary and didn't have a legal obligation to work in their best interests, I could recommend two different but comparable products. Product A had higher expenses and paid me a 5 percent commission, and Product B had much lower expenses, so it only paid me a 1 percent commission.

You can see the conflict and dilemma. I could recommend Product B and make $10,000 ($1 million × 1 percent) or Product A and make five times that amount, or $50,000 ($1 million × 5 percent)! Even though the higher-cost product wasn't best for a client, which one was I incentivized to sell? Back then, fees were rarely disclosed or discussed.

We started the firm to avoid these types of conflicts, to be objective, and to work only as a fiduciary to clients. It also meant we had to disclose all our compensation. We were confident our clients would appreciate our independence and transparency. Knowing our advice was only merit-based and in their best interest immediately built trust with our clients.

We spotted this trend early, and it's worked well over the past fifteen-plus years. We've grown from a team of two people managing about $15 million in assets to twenty-five employees advising assets of more than $4.5 billion at the end of 2019.

When we started the firm, we only worked with individual clients, providing comprehensive financial planning and discretionary portfolio management. Several private clients at Greenspring were small business owners. As part of the financial planning process, we would check the investment options in their 401(k) plan. From what I saw, these options were a mess. They were almost always actively managed and expensive. The menu of options looked like there wasn't any intelligent, thoughtful design to them either.

Digging into the fees, there was little transparency as well. It was challenging to determine the true costs, and the conflicts of interest I saw were frightening.

Feeling like our fiduciary model and passive, index-focused investment philosophy we used for our clients could disrupt the 401(k) space, I recognized an opportunity. I thought I might even build a successful retirement plan consulting practice. So my co-founder Pat Collins and I agreed that I would focus on trying to find 401(k) opportunities. There was only one problem: I had no real experience.

Before Greenspring, I worked for one of the largest brokerage firms in the world and worked with a single 401(k) plan. I knew nothing about these types of plans and didn't understand what I was doing. I've come a long way since then, and so has Greenspring. Back then, it was 2006, and few advisory firms were promoting the concept of fiduciary responsibility. I believed we could use this to differentiate ourselves since it was a cornerstone of our firm. I began to ask lots of people in the industry what they knew about ERISA fiduciary responsibility. Few people had more than a cursory knowledge of the concept. One afternoon, I printed out the entire ERISA regulation and read it over a weekend. This solidified my belief that most people had no clue what it meant to be a fiduciary.

I came across Fred Reish, one of the retirement industry's most well-known ERISA attorneys and read everything I could find that he'd written. About six weeks later, I had developed a solid foundation of fiduciary knowledge. And I realized I knew much more than most people I came across.

I developed my philosophy on what a successful retirement plan looked like. It began with the idea that every great retirement plan started with a strong retirement committee and a sound fiduciary process. That's because these were the people who controlled almost every important retirement plan decision in a company. Employees had little control—only deciding whether to participate, how much to contribute, and which investments to choose based on a handful of preselected options. Otherwise, the plan fiduciaries made all the major decisions. They selected the investments, determined the fees, chose the plan features, and hired the vendors who supported the plan. Yet I found few companies that had a strong, formal retirement committee and a comprehensive governance process in place.

In most cases, the prospective clients I came across didn't know what they didn't know. I sensed an opportunity. My mission became helping companies create high-performance retirement committees. I began discussing things like a committee charter, fiduciary appointment letters, fiduciary training, an investment policy statement (IPS), meeting minutes, analyzing and benchmarking fees, eliminating revenue sharing, centralizing and storing plan documentation, and how an ERISA 3(38) fiduciary could help reduce risk.

My story was so different at the time (remember this was 2006) that few companies could understand it. Or perhaps I wasn't very good at telling it! Either way, I was dealing with a lot of rejection and often wanted to give up.

At one of my low points, I walked into Pat's office ready to throw in the towel. Pat talked me off the edge, and I'm so glad he did. I said I would write a book. He kind of laughed and asked me what I would call it. I said, "*Fixing the 401(k)* because this industry is broken!" I don't think he believed I would follow through on it, but that night, I went home and got to work, creating an outline. Over the next several months, I wrote on nights and weekends.

In August 2008, *Fixing the 401(k): What Fiduciaries Must Know (And Do) to Help Employees Retire Successfully* was published. That is still the single greatest investment I ever made in my career. It also helped set us on the course to where we are today. I immediately sent copies to three companies I had been prospecting for close to a year. Within a week, all three agreed to become clients. I began to speak at conferences around the country and to various groups, jumping at any chance I had to tell my story. Slowly, we started to build a client base.

In 2009, I made a good friend named Todd Lacey at an industry conference. Todd owned a similar firm in Athens, Georgia, called The (k)larity Group. We became close quickly and even kicked around the idea of merging our firms but held off. In late 2010, Todd texted me one night, asking if I wanted to buy his firm because he was taking a job with a top recordkeeper. In early 2011, we bought The (k)larity Group, adding an employee and about twenty-five plans. Suddenly, our client total was up to forty-five.

Later that year, I hired Matt Cellini. Matt had no retirement industry experience at the time but has now become one of the top advisors in the country. He's a partner at Greenspring, a gifted advisor, and a huge driver of our team's growth. In 2017, we added Greg Hobson as a partner and board member. Greg came to us from a large firm and has been a well-respected advisor in the industry for more than twenty years. He has become an integral part of our firm and success. I'd be remiss not to highlight the other members of our institutional team who have been a huge part of our growth, including Lauren Gwinn, Christian Stanley, Reiley Crosby, Molly Burton, Zack Hubbard, and Khaalid

Kamara. They are a talented, passionate, and knowledgeable team that goes above and beyond for our clients every day. I am proud to work with them.

Our institutional team now serves as a fiduciary to more than 115 plans. We advise clients on more than $3.6 billion in plan assets and serve the needs of close to 50,000 participants. On multiple occasions, we've been recognized as a PLANADVISER Top 100 Retirement Plan Adviser. And PLANSPONSOR named us the 2018 Retirement Plan Adviser of the Year—Small Team.

The retirement industry has significantly evolved in the last fifteen years. I've been honored to be a small part of the process that has brought about many of those changes, most importantly, championing the importance and virtue of fiduciary responsibility. But I'm not done. While it's simple to be a fiduciary, it's not easy to be an effective one, especially in a time when the role is becoming more difficult and complex.

Albert Einstein said that "most of the fundamental ideas of science are essentially simple, and may, as a rule, be expressed in a language comprehensible to everyone." I love that philosophy. In the pages that follow, I'm going to teach you the simple formula for creating the perfect retirement plan for the people who depend on you. I'm going to do what I can to make you the best fiduciary you can be.

CHAPTER 2

The Fiduciary Formula

I wasn't a very good chemistry student in high school. But one thing I remember is that elements are the simplest complete chemical substances that form the basic chemical building blocks of matter, each corresponding to a single entry on the periodic table.

There are 118 known elements. When two or more distinct elements are chemically bonded, the result is called a chemical compound. That compound is depicted using a chemical formula. For instance, water is a compound made from two elements: hydrogen and oxygen. The ratio of hydrogen atoms to oxygen atoms in water is always 2:1, so each molecule of water contains two hydrogen atoms bonded to a single oxygen atom and represented by the formula H_2O.

So here's how the Fiduciary Formula works. It helps me to think of comprehensive fiduciary governance like a chemical formula. You start with the six fiduciary elements that form the basis of any high-quality, high-performance corporate retirement plan. These elements correspond to the fiduciary periodic table:

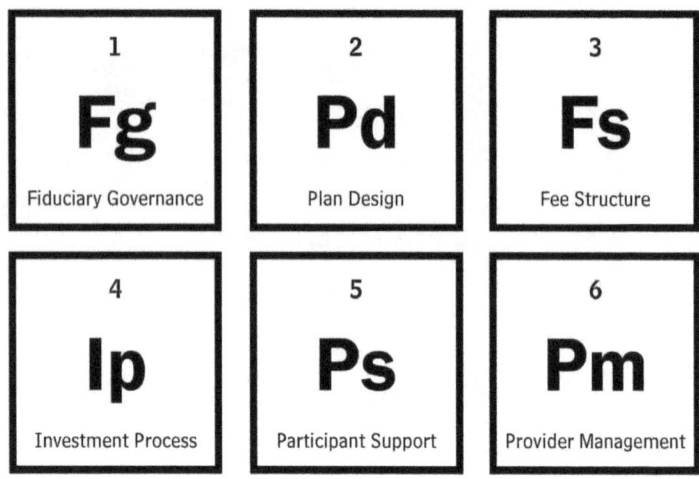

When you combine the six fiduciary elements, it creates the compound represented by the Fiduciary Formula:

For any science majors, you'll notice that the formula is slightly different than a standard chemical formula like H_2O. Since these fiduciary elements don't contain atoms, the subscript represents the number of elements that start with the corresponding letter. For instance, three of the six fiduciary elements are Plan Design, Participant Support, and Provider Management (or P_3).

I've divided this book into sections that correspond to each element, with several chapters dedicated to each section. I've tried to keep each chapter short and to the point. At the end of each section, you'll find a case study and a three-part summary for each fiduciary element that includes these icons:

Evidence

In writing the Fiduciary Formula, I've relied heavily on industry research and data. You will see the microscope symbol for evidence that I think is especially powerful.

Method

The beaker symbol represents what I call the Fiduciary Method, where I highlight new knowledge that can be applied to your plan or the plans you manage.

Questions

I've highlighted important questions throughout the book with the question mark symbol. Think of these as exam questions to help you think more deeply about the information covered.

Make no mistake, managing a corporate retirement plan is complex. At Greenspring Advisors, one of our trademarks is (k)larity, which we describe as making complex retirement decisions simple. We believe that (k)larity creates confidence.

Confidence comes from knowing what's important and what isn't. Confidence comes from being clear about what you want to accomplish, how to do it, and what success looks like. Confidence comes from developing knowledge, understanding, and mastery. Finally, confidence comes from seeing the long-term results of good decision-making.

Regardless of your role as part of the fiduciary ecosystem, I hope this book helps you develop a new sense of (k)larity and transforms the way you think about retirement plans. Now let's roll up our sleeves and get to work!

1

Fg

Fiduciary Governance

CHAPTER 3

———

It All Starts with the Committee (Fg)

A well-organized and effective retirement plan committee is the cornerstone of successful fiduciary decision-making and organizational risk management for plans of any size. However, great committees don't happen by accident—they are the product of a "best practices" approach to design and implementation. Most companies (especially smaller ones) skip this step or have ineffective informal committees. That's a major mistake for two reasons.

First, a highly engaged committee is the best indicator that a company cares about helping its employees retire successfully. A strong committee will make better decisions for employees, producing better results. This is important when we consider how little control employees have over their retirement experience. They control whether they will participate (and at what level) and how to invest their money given a limited set of preselected choices. It's the company that makes almost all the decisions and sets the game up for people, choosing the vendors; the level and structure of fees; the number, types, and quality of investments made available; what options and features are included from a plan design perspective; the level of plan funding; and what services to make available to assist employees. These factors will almost entirely determine whether your employees have a successful retirement. Said another way: your employees, your friends, your colleagues, and their families are relying on you to make the best decisions for them. Second, without a strong committee, it's unlikely your organization is implementing a comprehensive and consistent fiduciary oversight process. By failing to do so, you create unnecessary risks for yourself and the organization. What if a fiduciary breach occurs and employees bring costly and time-consuming litigation? Or what if an enforcement action comes from the Department of Labor or an operational failure occurs that needs correcting? In my experience, fiduciary litigation by participants is rare (though high profile). While it's always possible, it's improbable. Enforcement actions and operational failures are far more common, posing a greater risk for companies. The Employee Benefits Security Administration (EBSA) at the US Department of Labor (DOL) routinely publishes the results of its activities as the agency responsible for investigating and enforcing the fiduciary duties under the Employee Retirement Income Security Act of 1974 (ERISA). In 2019, EBSA recovered $2.5 billion, including $2.02 billion in enforcement actions. In getting these monetary results, EBSA closed 1,146 civil investigations, with 67 percent of these cases resulting in monetary recoveries or other corrective action and 89 cases referred for litigation.[1]

While an effective committee that follows a comprehensive and consistent process doesn't eliminate the possibility of a fiduciary breach or an operational failure, it minimizes the chance of either. And it increases the likelihood that operational failures will be identified and resolved quickly, minimizing the associated costs and pain.

I want to make an important point relating to managing fiduciary risk. The primary goal of sound fiduciary governance is to increase the probability of successful retirement outcomes for employees. The by-product, or secondary goal, should be fiduciary risk management. If you focus on the first issue, the second issue will take care of itself.

In the next two chapters, I will show you how you can develop a high-performance retirement plan committee.

CHAPTER 4

Developing and Equipping
Your Committee (Fg)

Your first step is choosing the right number of committee members. In my experience, the most effective committees have between three and seven members. Too few members limit the diversity of thought and the ability to achieve a quorum. Too many members can lead to ineffectiveness as it's difficult to gain consensus with too many cooks in the kitchen.

Contrary to popular opinion, members need not be investment or retirement plan experts, but they should be committed, engaged, and have a reputation for making good decisions. Typically, finance and HR are represented on the committee, and a member from legal may be included, depending on the size of the organization. In most cases, committee members are appointed by the board of directors.

Next, appoint a chairperson and a secretary. Strong committees have strong leadership. The chairperson's job is to ensure the committee meets regularly and to facilitate those meetings. It's a crucial role, as they have the final authority on decisions when the committee reaches an impasse. The secretary's job is to distribute all relevant information to members and to document committee business (e.g., meeting minutes).

Last, utilize a committee charter. A misunderstanding of the group's roles and responsibilities undercuts many committees. A committee charter is a short document that serves as a mission statement for the committee. It outlines what the group is accountable for and identifies procedures for removing or replacing members. Each person on the committee should either sign this document or a fiduciary acknowledgment letter, accepting their appointment to the committee and acknowledging they understand their duties and responsibilities.

Providing comprehensive fiduciary training is one of the most important things a company can do to best equip its retirement plan committee members. This important step minimizes fiduciary risk through education and governance.

While the DOL views fiduciary training as a critical element of prudent oversight and looks for evidence that fiduciary training has been provided during plan audits, formal fiduciary training is still rare within the industry. In 2017, Xponential Growth Solutions conducted a survey of 977 plan sponsors and found that nearly 70 percent had received no formal fiduciary training. A breakdown of the responses, both by plan type and size, are highlighted here.

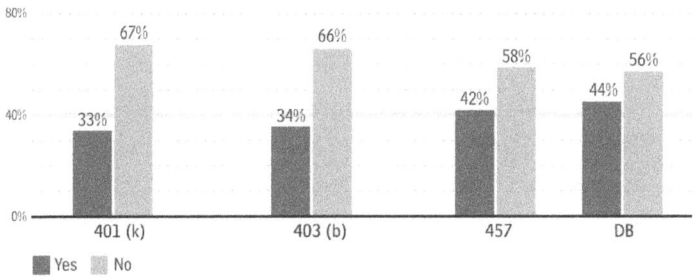

Fiduciary Training By Plan Type

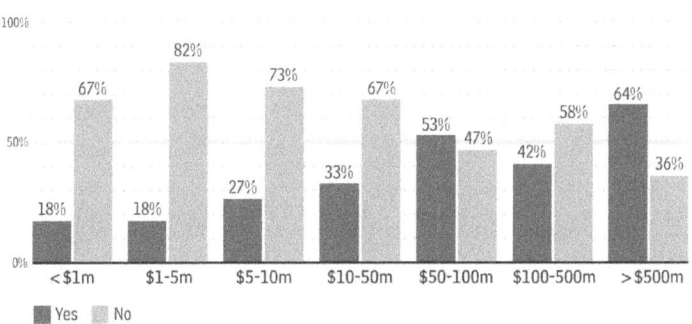

Fiduciary Training By Plan Size

Once you've selected and appointed committee members, you should provide fiduciary training. This training should be completed by committee members each year. Here are ten areas that form the foundation of a comprehensive fiduciary training curriculum:

1. **Overview of ERISA**—Covers the history and background of ERISA and which plans are subject to the regulation.
2. **Fiduciary Status and Duties**—Reviews fiduciary versus nonfiduciary functions and ERISA's fiduciary duties and elements of a prudent process.
3. **Fiduciary Liability**—Discusses common fiduciary breach claims, consequences of a breach, and prohibited transactions.
4. **Plan Management**—Addresses various aspects of the plan

document, amendments, Form 5500, and participant disclosures.

5. **Plan Investments**—Describes investment duties under ERISA, selection and monitoring best practices, and 404(c) protection.

6. **Plan Fees**—Covers fee types, allocation methods, revenue sharing, and administrative versus settlor expenses.

7. **Vendor Selection and Management**—Reviews how to properly evaluate and select vendors and service providers and outsourced 3(16) administrative services.

8. **Hot Topics for Fiduciaries**—Discusses fee litigation, DOL and IRS enforcement priorities, and target date fund (TDF) selection.

9. **Litigation Lessons**—Describes several landmark court decisions that provide real-life lessons about the importance of a prudent fiduciary process.

10. **Other Issues and Best Practices**—Addresses bonding and insurance, fiduciary governance/oversight structure, and the need for fiduciary process documentation.

In my experience, fiduciary expertise is best provided by a knowledgeable, third-party expert. Fiduciary U (FiduciaryU.com) includes an online fiduciary training curriculum developed in consultation with one of the country's leading ERISA attorneys, Fred Reish. It's a comprehensive and cost-effective way to train retirement plan fiduciaries.

Next, you'll want your committee to develop an investment policy statement (IPS). An IPS describes the process for selecting and monitoring plan investments while showing a prudent fiduciary process is being followed. It's an essential tool in the fiduciary's toolbox, and we'll discuss its importance in more depth in later chapters.

Last, you'll want to purchase fiduciary liability insurance. Fiduciaries can be held personally liable under ERISA for losses to a retirement plan incurred because of their alleged errors, omissions, or breaches in fiduciary duties.

While not required by ERISA and not a substitute for a sound fiduciary process, fiduciary liability insurance protects against fiduciary-related claims of employee benefit plan mismanagement. It also covers the legal expenses of defending against fiduciary breach of duty claims and limits financial losses the plan sponsor may incur. It's permissible (and advisable) for employers and fiduciaries to maintain liability insurance covering fiduciary breach and similar claims under ERISA. If the policy isn't unique to ERISA, employers and fiduciaries should make sure their policies cover breach claims since many general insurance policies may not.

The amount of advisable coverage differs from case to case, though a general rule of thumb is coverage for 5 percent of plan assets and 10 percent if employer stock is an investment option. It's also permissible for an employer to indemnify (i.e., agree to satisfy any liability on behalf of) their plan fiduciaries. Any indemnification must be paid from corporate assets, never plan assets. Employers and fiduciaries should discuss this issue, including the precise scope of any indemnification, and ensure that the policy is permissible under ERISA. You may also want to purchase employee benefits liability insurance (EBLI), which offers financial protection from lawsuits and claims stemming from company errors or mismanagement regarding the administration of your retirement plan (and/or other benefit plans). Your insurance agent or broker can help you decide whether to purchase these coverages.

CHAPTER 5

———

Engaging Your Committee (Fg)

Once you've developed and equipped your committee, it's time to get to work. First and foremost, your committee should meet regularly. There's no meeting frequency requirement in ERISA, but every committee should meet at least annually or semiannually. Larger plans typically meet quarterly. If well organized, these meetings shouldn't take more than one to two hours. It's also a good idea to schedule meetings at the beginning of the year, getting the dates on everyone's calendar as soon as possible.

Using an accountability calendar to map out the key deliverables to cover throughout the year (e.g., fee analysis, investment monitoring, plan benchmark, plan design review, etc.) is a great way to organize your efforts and ensure all bases are being covered in the most efficient way possible. Here's an example of how quarterly meetings could be structured:

Q1

1. Prior Year Plan Accomplishments and Milestones
2. Industry Trends
3. Current Year Goal Setting
4. New Tools and Deliverables
5. Annual Calendar Review
6. Investment Review
7. Fee Analysis

Q2

1. Fiduciary Training
2. Fiduciary Checklist Best Practices
3. IPS and Charter Review
4. Legislative and Regulatory Update
5. Investment Review
6. Fee Analysis

Q3

1. Fund Lineup Review
2. Target Date Fund Deep Dive
3. Market Insights
4. Fee Benchmark
5. Investment Review
6. Fee Analysis

Q4

1. Participant Demographics
2. Employee Survey Review
3. Engagement/Utilization Review
4. Investment Review
5. Fee Analysis

With ERISA, the best defense for retirement committees is always a strong offense. Taking official minutes at each meeting is a cornerstone practice to conform to mandated ERISA requirements. Failure to take minutes is evidence of a poorly constructed fiduciary governance process that can lead to ERISA litigation, which is on the rise and discussed in chapter 11. Just remember, it's been said the DOL and courts take the position that if it wasn't documented, it didn't happen.

Let's look more closely at the actual benefits of meeting minutes:

- Your committee has a structured format for documenting your decision-making process in a concise and well-organized way.
- Your committee has a method to review and audit historical decisions and outcomes over time, which is beneficial for existing and new committee members.
- Your committee possesses an official record that can support the facts surrounding your decision-making process in a court of law.

Effective minutes should identify which members were present, what information was reviewed and discussed, any decisions that were made along with the competing factors considered, and the key reasons for the decisions. Effective minutes are crafted to be beneficial, not detrimental, in a court of law. A list of action items, including time frames and responsible parties, should also be included. You should incorporate input and reports from third-party experts as appropriate. Last, at each meeting, you should review the minutes from the previous meeting to make sure any outstanding items have been completed.

Taking minutes at every meeting might seem simple, but it's not easy. Committees often fail to take minutes for a variety of reasons:

- The company doesn't have a formal retirement committee, so no meetings take place.
- There is technically a retirement committee, but it meets infrequently and without a defined structure or format.
- The committee doesn't realize it should take minutes, and none of its service providers have recommended it (which means they are not working with specialists or the right partners).
- No one on the committee or with one of the service providers has been assigned the responsibility or taken the initiative to take minutes.

Any of these inadvertent failures can be fixed with the right combination of focus and discipline. At our firm, we take ownership of creating the initial draft of meeting minutes as part of our client service process, which is reviewed and approved by the committee.

Holding on to minutes is almost as important as taking them in the first place. Plan documentation needs to be kept for significant periods of time. ERISA's general statute of limitations period for breach claims is six years, and breach claims may often implicate decisions made even further in the past, sometimes ten or more years. ERISA also requires fiduciaries to maintain records to support Form 5500 information for six years from the filing date.

Therefore, it's a good idea to maintain a fiduciary file for organization and record retention purposes. A fiduciary file serves as the central location for all plan-related information, taking the guesswork out of organizing and maintaining plan records. It also ensures all processes are documented and meet ERISA standards. While hard copies of information are sufficient, leveraging technology to manage the fiduciary process can yield significant benefits in terms of time management, consistency of execution, and ease of access.

Investing the time to develop, equip, and engage a high-performance retirement plan committee is a key to managing risk and running a successful plan. Over time, implementing these best practices should enhance the consistency and quality of decision-making, drive successful outcomes, and increase the probability that your employees will retire with dignity.

CASE STUDY

Onboarding a new client is a lot of work, but it's a great time to create a strong fiduciary foundation. As a former Division I and minor league player, I like to think of this process using a baseball analogy. Major League Baseball teams don't start the season right away. They use spring training to practice and get in shape for a long, grueling 162-game season. Once we get under contract with a new client, we schedule a kickoff meeting with the committee. This kickoff meeting is like spring training for the committee.

During that initial meeting, we typically draft three important documents. The first is a sample board resolution for the company to use that delegate's authority for plan oversight to the committee and authorizes the creation of a committee charter. The second document is a draft of the committee charter itself that formalizes the committee (including the appointment of a chairperson and secretary). It also outlines the duties and responsibilities for the group, as well as the roles of individual members. Last, we create a draft of the investment policy statement (IPS).

Together, we spend time walking through each document and answering any questions the committee has. The committee is instructed to review the document after the meeting and customize the board resolution and charter to the specific needs of their company. Once these are finalized, all three documents are executed.

Next, we provide an introduction to ERISA's basic fiduciary duties and responsibilities, and we send access to our comprehensive fiduciary training course as a follow-up to the meeting, strongly recommending each member take our online course.

We then set up the client's fiduciary file and upload any existing documentation along with these newly executed documents.

Finally, we schedule the upcoming year's committee meetings so it's on everyone's calendar, and we ensure a consistent meeting rhythm.

Once these steps are finished, spring training is officially over, and the season begins!

1

Fg

Fiduciary Governance

SUMMARY

- In 2019, EBSA recovered $2.5 billion, including $2.02 billion in enforcement actions. In getting these monetary results, EBSA closed 1,146 civil investigations, with 67 percent of these cases resulting in monetary recoveries or other corrective action, and 89 cases referred for litigation.
- A 2017 survey of 977 plan sponsors by Xponential Growth Solutions found that nearly 70 percent had received no formal fiduciary training.

- Create a formal retirement committee with three to seven members.
- Use a committee charter.

- Develop and follow an IPS.
- Provide annual fiduciary training to committee members.
- Use an accountability calendar for annual meeting rhythms.
- Have one to two committee meetings per year for smaller plans and two to four meetings for larger plans.
- Take meeting minutes.
- Use a fiduciary file.

1. Do you have a retirement committee?
2. How often does the committee meet?
3. Do you have between three and seven members?
4. Have members been formally appointed by the board of directors?
5. Do you have a committee charter?
6. Have members been provided fiduciary training each year?
7. Do you have a formal IPS?
8. Do you take minutes of every meeting?
9. Do you have a fiduciary file?
10. Do you use an accountability calendar?
11. Are meetings scheduled at the beginning of the year to ensure they are on everyone's calendars ahead of time?

2

Pd

Plan Design

CHAPTER 6

─────

Behavioral Finance
Concepts (Pd)

Did you know more than 21,000 women are expected to be diagnosed with ovarian cancer in 2020, and nearly 14,000 women will lose their lives to this deadly disease? It ranks fifth in cancer deaths among women, and the risk of getting ovarian cancer during a woman's lifetime is about one in seventy-eight.[2]

I know this because my mom is a forty-five-year survivor of ovarian cancer, having been diagnosed extremely early because of my birth. Being in her late twenties, combined with this early diagnosis, was critical to her treatment, her recovery, and her remission.

The overall five-year survival rate of ovarian cancer is 48 percent,[3] but this varies widely, depending on the extent or stage of the cancer and the age of the woman. If the cancer is diagnosed and treated before it has spread outside the ovaries, the five-year survival rate is 92 percent. However, if it has spread to the surrounding organs or tissue (known as regional spread), the five-year survival rate is 75 percent. And if the cancer has spread to parts of the body far away from the ovaries (known as distant spread), the five-year survival rate drops to 29 percent. My mom was lucky because her cancer was diagnosed before it had spread. That's why she's still with us today.

So what does this have to do with retirement? Well, it's a fact that we have an impending retirement savings crisis. In the words of former Federal Reserve chairman Ben Bernanke, "The arithmetic, unfortunately, is quite clear." If people's savings behavior doesn't significantly change, they won't make it. In this way, it's much like a cancer diagnosis for people's financial future. There are many people who fall into the terminal category, and the best we can hope for them is to make life a little more comfortable and tolerable. But time is the great healer, and there are many still in the early stages. For them, there's time to take aggressive savings action and a great chance they'll be able to enjoy a long and healthy financial life in retirement.

In the next few chapters, I will discuss the aggressive treatment methods that are necessary and effective for curing retirement cancer.

According to the Employee Benefit Research Institute's (EBRI's) 2017 Retirement Confidence Survey, only 18 percent of workers surveyed were very confident about having enough money for a comfortable retirement, 42 percent were only somewhat confident, 24 percent were not too confident, and a whopping 16 percent weren't at all confident.[4] Unpacking those numbers, we find nearly half of all people surveyed were seriously worried about their retirement chances.

So let's take a step back for a moment and gain a little perspective in terms of the roles and responsibilities of plan fiduciaries to help employees retire successfully. Section 404 of ERISA outlines the basic fiduciary duties, including the "exclusive purpose of (i) providing benefits to participants and their beneficiaries and defraying reasonable expense of administering the plan."[5] Put another way, as a fiduciary, you should be making decisions that put your participants in the best position to accumulate the most money possible at the lowest reasonable cost. I've found many fiduciaries don't understand this is the job description. Others simply don't want to believe it. Belief is important here. If you believe something, you align your decisions and your actions with those beliefs. I am a passionate and vocal proponent of plan design features such as automatic enrollment, automatic escalation, and default investing. Automatic features have had a tremendous impact on retirement outcomes over the past ten years. For instance, in Vanguard's *How America Saves 2019* annual report, the fund company and retirement vendor found the following at the end of 2018:

- Nearly six in ten of all Vanguard participants were solely invested in an automatic investment program (such as a target date fund, managed account, or balanced fund), compared with just one in ten at the end of 2004. This number is projected to increase to 80 percent by year-end 2023.
- The adoption of automatic enrollment across its client base has tripled since year-end 2007. For instance, 48 percent of Vanguard plans had adopted automatic enrollment as opposed to just 15 percent at the end of 2007.
- Aggressive default rates (5-plus percent) have increased substantially. At the end of 2009, only 16 percent of Vanguard's clients had a default rate of 5 percent or more, but by the end of 2018, that number had increased to 38 percent.
- At the end of 2018, the average participation rate for automatic enrollment plans was 91 percent versus only 60 percent for plans requiring voluntary enrollment.

Here's a good starting point for employers: aim for a minimum of 90 percent plan participation, at least 10 percent in total annual retirement contributions per employee, and having at least 90 percent of employees invested in a professionally managed vehicle, such as a target date fund or managed account. The key here is that these percentages should be the floor, not the ceiling. Taking steps to address these three areas is probably the single most impactful thing any company can do for its employees and their financial future.

This is more commonly known as the 90-10-90 rule as outlined by Dr. Shlomo Benartzi and shared in his book *Save More Tomorrow*. Dr. Benartzi is a behavioral economist and a professor and co-founder of the Behavioral Decision-Making Group at UCLA Anderson School of Management. His research, conducted with Dr. Richard Thaler of the University of Chicago (and the 2017 recipient of the Nobel Memorial Prize in Economic Sciences for his contributions to behavioral economics), was instrumental in the adoption of automatic plan features that were incorporated into the Pension Protection Act of 2006.

Speaking of behavioral research, let's look at an interesting social science experiment. I came across this experiment in Daniel Pink's book *To Sell Is Human: The Surprising Truth About Moving Others*, which is a fantastic read if you have any responsibility for leading, motivating, or influencing people.

In 2011, a group of researchers led by a social psychologist named Hal Hershfield conducted a fascinating series of experiments to determine barriers that keep people from saving.

The concept of saving for retirement seems simple, and you would expect most rational people to both realize they need to save and to do it. It's a tradeoff between immediate rewards versus future rewards. However, our brains are wired in a way that makes us terrible at choosing rewards we have to wait for, and we often choose immediate rewards even when we know it's not in our best interest. Think about the adage "A bird in the hand is worth two in the bush."

As part of the experiment, the researchers used computer animation to show people a digital avatar of themselves (i.e., their current self) and what they would conceivably look like at age seventy (i.e., their future self). They had half the participants use a virtual reality headset in which they saw their current-self avatar for about a minute and then had a short conversation with a researcher's digital representation. The second group followed the same process, except they saw their future selves instead of their current selves.

Afterward, the experimenters told all the participants to imagine they had unexpectedly received $1,000, and they had to allocate the money among four different options: buying something nice for someone special, investing it in a retirement fund, planning a fun and extravagant occasion, or putting it in a checking account. The group who saw their current selves saved an average of $80 in the retirement account. However, the group that saw their future selves allocated $172 to the retirement account. That's more than twice the amount of the current-self group!

Next, the researchers wanted to see what drove that difference—participants seeing themselves as older or just aging in general. Using a different group of participants, they followed a very similar process, except half the participants saw an age-morphed picture of themselves while the other half saw an age-morphed picture of someone else.

The results were clear—those who saw the seventy-year-old picture of themselves saved significantly more than those who simply saw a picture of some random seventy-year-old. The issue isn't just our inability to weigh immediate versus future rewards; it's the fact that we often feel a disconnection from our future selves, as though they are an entirely different person.

In the research paper, Hershfield and his colleagues stated that "to people estranged from their future selves, saving is like a choice between spending money today and giving it to a stranger years from now." However, showing people an image of themselves getting old helped foster that psychological connection, causing them to save more.

The results of this study have all sorts of interesting implications. But one thing I think it highlights is the inability and ineffectiveness of trying to convince participants to save more. As an industry, we spend incredible amounts of time and money trying to educate people and get them to better balance short-term and long-term rewards. Sadly, little incremental impact is being made.

Think about the shiny brochures and educational materials we give people. The ones with pictures of smiling older faces looking healthy and happy in retirement. Given the results from this study, is it any wonder this information doesn't sink in and change the behavior of most participants? As you will see, the traditional approach to plan design is very ineffective at overcoming the behavioral inertia that keeps people from saving for retirement. Alternatively, automatic plan design uses that inertia *for* participants as opposed to *against* them.

CHAPTER 7

Focusing on Replacement Rates (Pd)

Let's change gears and talk about income replacement rates. The retirement income challenge is a math equation. If we can identify the projected amount of money needed with some level of confidence, we can then work backward and use a person's current assets along with their sources of income and assumptions about projected rates of return to solve for the level of annual savings required.

In 2012, two researchers with Dimensional Fund Advisors, Dr. Marlena Lee and Dr. Massi De Santis, attempted to project the replacement rates needed by retirees as a percentage of gross preretirement income.[6] Their analysis included the breakdown between Social Security and personal savings, such as pension income and 401(k) assets, IRAs, and so forth. They simulated income and portfolio paths for 100,000 households using the working years between ages twenty-five to sixty-five, with full retirement occurring at age sixty-six.

According to their results, lower-income workers were projected to need a *higher* overall replacement rate but a *lower* percentage coming from personal retirement savings. This is because Social Security made up a higher percentage of replacement income for people at this income level.

Workers with income in the bottom quartile who made less than approximately $26,000 per year were projected to have to replace 82 percent of their preretirement income. Social Security was expected to contribute 59 percent, while 23 percent needed to come from personal retirement savings.

At the other end of the spectrum, those who were in the highest income quartile and made more than $86,000 per year had a lower overall projected replacement rate (58 percent), but Social Security contributed a much smaller percentage at only 21 percent. This meant the worker would need to replace nearly 37 percent of their preretirement income through personal retirement savings.

For the analysis, the researchers projected that the typical worker would need to replace somewhere between 20 and 40 percent of preretirement income from their own savings, depending on income level. Here were the total projected savings rates needed per year based on the probability of success using Monte Carlo simulations. Since these were total savings, they would include any employer contributions.

	Savings Rate	
Success Probability	**40% Replacement**	**20% Replacement**
95%	16.8%	8.4%
90%	13.2%	6.6%
50%	5.2%	2.6%

Source: Dimensional Fund Advisors (DFA). Results based on Monte Carlo simulations of income profiles, stock returns, and bond returns for 100,000 households. Income profiles calibrated using PSID data and census data. Stock and bond returns bootstrapped using historical returns.

For instance, a higher-paid employee who started saving at age twenty-five and needed to replace 40 percent of their income would need to average total savings rates of 16.8 percent to have a 95 percent confidence level. At a 5.2 percent total savings rate, the outcome was a coin toss.

Similarly, a lower-paid employee who started saving at age twenty-five and needed to replace 20 percent of their income would need to average total savings rates of 8.4 percent to reach a 95 percent confidence level.

If someone is lucky enough to have an employer pension, that will take some pressure off the level of personal savings needed. But in this day and age, pension income is rare, which means most of the current and future generations of workers will need to replace nearly all of this income through personal savings alone.

Further, in these simulations, it's important to realize workers began saving at age twenty-five to reach the projected outcomes. Starting early is crucial. Think of this as an early diagnosis in my cancer example from the last chapter.

This chart illustrates the detrimental impact of waiting to save.

Postponing retirement savings for five additional years (to age thirty) required annual savings increases of nearly 3 percent. Those who waited ten years to start saving needed to increase the annual savings rate by 7 percent.

Success Probability	Start at 25	Start at 30	Start at 35
95%	16.8%	19.5%	23.8%
90%	13.2%	15.4%	19.2%
50%	5.2%	6.4%	8.7%

Source: Dimensional Fund Advisors (DFA). Results based on Monte Carlo simulations of income profiles, stock returns, and bond returns for 100,000 households. Income profiles calibrated using PSID data and census data. Stock and bond returns bootstrapped using historical returns.

CHAPTER 8

———

Adoption of Automatic Features (Pd)

I've made the case that we have a retirement savings crisis. As we've seen, people aren't wired to save effectively. That means savings rates need to be much higher to make the arithmetic work.

But how do we do that? Fear not. It is doable. There are levers you can pull to supercharge your plan participation and savings rates and get your people on the path to retirement success. Let's look more closely at how plan fiduciaries can help by examining automatic plan features.

AUTOMATIC ENROLLMENT

According to *PLANSPONSOR* magazine, roughly 48 percent of all plans use automatic enrollment.[7] Within the industry, the largest plans tend to be early adopters of research, trends, and best practices, and you can see this at work. Large plans use automatic enrollment at a rate of nearly three to one over the smallest plans.

One of the biggest challenges people face when saving for retirement is having to voluntarily enroll in their plan. If someone isn't participating in a plan, they can't save. Automatic enrollment has been a huge success in driving increased plan participation. In the third quarter of 2019, Fidelity found that participation rates in voluntary plans across its client base averaged 52.3 percent, while participation in automatic enrollment plans averaged 88.3 percent![8]

Many plan sponsors think automatic enrollment won't be effective for younger and lower-income workers. In fact, the opposite is true. Vanguard's *How America Saves 2019* annual report found employees earning $15,000 to $30,000 participated at a rate of only 38 percent across its client base when required to voluntarily enroll.[9] When automatically enrolled, these employees participated at a rate of 88 percent. Among those under age twenty-five, voluntary participation was only 18 percent, compared to 82 percent when automatically enrolled.

Remember how crucial starting early is? The best thing you can do for the financial future of your younger workers is to automatically enroll them. Still, the data suggests that it's never too late and that inertia isn't an age thing. Workers over age sixty-five participated at a rate of only 62 percent when forced to enroll as compared to 88 percent when automatically enrolled.

DEFAULT PERCENTAGE

Once you've decided to implement automatic enrollment, you must choose a default percentage. According to PLANSPONSOR, the most common default is 3 percent (used by 38 percent of plans).[10] However, this trend is changing, and plan sponsors are getting more aggressive in their default percentages. For instance,

T. Rowe Price has seen the percentage of plans with a default savings rate of 6 percent or more increase from 18.7 percent in 2012 to 36.9 percent in 2018.[11]

I believe in setting the default to at least 6 percent. That will get your employees on track much faster and put them further ahead in their savings goals. It is the rate I recommend to my clients and is the default for our own plan at Greenspring Advisors.

In our 2019 employee financial wellness and well-being survey (which I discuss in more detail in chapters 21 to 23), we asked nearly 1,900 workers what they thought was the "ideal" default percentage. Forty percent of all employees felt the ideal should be at least 6 percent, while 60 percent felt it should be at least 5 percent.[12]

Preferences aside, we also asked employees what they would do if they were defaulted at a percentage both above and below what they listed as ideal. Of those who were defaulted above their ideal, 48 percent said they would stay at the percentage or increase it further. For those who were defaulted below their ideal, 63 percent said they would increase the percentage to what they selected as ideal, and 15 percent said they would increase it above the default. T. Rowe Price found similar statistics in 2018, when only 6.9 percent of automatically enrolled participants decreased their default deferral rate.[13]

In both scenarios, only 6 percent of respondents said they would opt out and stop participating. This illustrates that the people who will opt out will do so no matter what level you set the default, so you might as well set it higher rather than lower.

Participants always have the choice to opt out, but most won't. If automatic enrollment caused significant frustration for employees, you'd see much higher opt-out rates. If you're serious about helping your people retire, you'll do everything you can to put them on the right path as quickly as possible, and that means automatically enrolling them at a meaningful rate.

There is a potential negative side effect of automatic enrollment, however. While automatic enrollment drives much higher *participation* rates, it can lead to lower average *deferral* rates when the default is set too low. For instance, if you add many people to the plan at 3 percent and they stay there, they will bring down the average deferral. That's because people get stuck at or around the default rate unless there's a mechanism to automatically increase their deferrals.

AUTOMATIC ESCALATION

It's important to pair automatic escalation with automatic enrollment to combat the trend of participants getting stuck at or around the default and to help them increase their saving rate over time. Automatic escalation increases a participant's contribution rate each year by 1 to 2 percent, unless they opt out. As a common practice, it's often coordinated with raises and merit increases because participants will feel less of an impact.

According to PLANSPONSOR, automatic escalation is used at a lower rate than automatic enrollment, however, with 23 percent of plans using the feature. Much like automatic enrollment, the largest plans utilize automatic escalation at a rate of almost six to one over the smallest plans.[14]

Many plans use the opt-in adoption method for automatic escalation instead of the opt-out method. With the opt-in method, a participant has to voluntarily elect to be automatically increased, whereas the opt-out method means they will be automatically increased. The opt-in method is much less effective, and I don't recommend it.

For example, T. Rowe Price found that participant usage of escalation was 458 percent higher with the opt-out method (67 percent versus 12 percent). It all goes back to behavioral inertia.

A final consideration when implementing automatic escalation is what level to set the cap, or the percentage that increases will stop. According to Vanguard, at the end of 2018, only 32 percent of plans had an escalation cap of 11 percent or higher, and 46 percent stopped escalating once a default rate of 10 percent was achieved.

However, I believe in setting the cap much higher, to at least 15 percent. A 2010 research report by the Employee Benefit Research Institute (EBRI) and the Defined Contribution Institutional Investment Association (DCIIA) found that the simple decision to set the automatic escalation cap at 15 percent increased the probability of achieving an 80 percent replacement rate by 16.4 percent for the lowest-income workers and 14.1 percent for the highest-income workers.[15] By far, this had the greatest impact of any single factor on increasing the probability of success.

PARTICIPANT INVESTING TRENDS

In combination with implementing automatic enrollment, it's necessary to choose a default investment option, such as a target date fund (TDF), a managed account, or a balanced fund for participants. These types of investments are known as a Qualified Default Investment Alternative (QDIA).

According to Morningstar, TDF assets have increased almost tenfold from December 2007 to December 2018, growing from $180 billion to $1.7 trillion.[16] Target date funds are projected to capture 85 cents of every new dollar contributed to 401(k) plans by 2021.[17] I believe QDIA selection is the single-most important investment decision our generation of fiduciaries will make for participants. It's also important to recognize participant investing trends, and despite the considerable efforts to make people better do-it-yourself (DIY) investors, the evidence suggests it's never worked very well now or in the past.

According to a Fidelity survey, nearly eight in ten participants said they didn't have the skill, will, or time to manage their invest-ments.[18] And yet, upon further analysis, six of ten participants were invested as a DIYer but hadn't sought guidance or changed their portfolio in two years or more.[19] That major disconnect is why many DIYers have unsuccessful investment experiences.

In *Fixing the 401(k)*, I cited a longitudinal study from 1997 to 2006 that compared the returns of approximately 15,000 participants who were DIY investors versus those who used a professionally managed option, like a lifestyle fund or a target date fund. Those in the professionally managed options earned 1.9 percent higher returns per year over the ten-year period than DIYers. These inves-tors ended the period with 11 percent higher account balances. Also, nearly 85 percent of DIYers would have been better off in a professionally managed portfolio.[20]

JPMorgan analyzed target date fund investors across its client base from 2008 to 2013, a particularly difficult time period because it included the Great Recession. Most investors get themselves in trouble by doing the wrong thing at the wrong time, which can be exacerbated in periods of market volatility and stress. They compared TDF users to DIYers who either used core menu funds or self-directed brokerage accounts.

Standardized 5-Year Returns	TDF User	DIYer	Brokerage User
High	19.8%	27.7%	26.5%
Median	13.9%	12.9%	12.4%
Low	8.5%	–2.2%	–1.8%

Source: JPMorgan Retirement Plan Services proprietary research. The analysis measurement period is December 31, 2008, through December 31, 2013. The data represents a sampling of participant data. It does not represent the returns of any individual product or portfolio.

On average, TDF users had returns that were 1 to 1.5 percent higher per year during this period than DIYers. More important, I think, is the range of returns. While the most successful DIYers and brokerage users had higher returns, the least successful investors struggled. In comparison, the range of returns for TDF users was much tighter, and those TDF investors on the low end outperformed comparable DIYers by more than 10 percent.

When my daughter Lydia was in kindergarten, I took her to a classmate's birthday party at a local bowling alley. The owners of the bowling alley were smart. To make sure all the kids had a fun and successful experience, they put up bumpers so no one would throw a gutter ball. The kids had a blast because they were knocking down pins left and right. As soon as we got in the car, my daughter said she wanted to have a bowling birthday party. Score one for the bowling alley owners (especially given how expensive it is to bowl these days)!

My fiduciary philosophy is that you should engineer every area of your plan (e.g., plan design, fees, investments, etc.) with your *least* sophisticated employee in mind and do all you can to keep them from throwing a proverbial gutter ball with their retirement savings. I believe that target date funds, while not a perfect solution or the right option for everyone, are the best investment solution for most participants, who are likely to be disengaged at some level.

Once you identify the right target date fund for your plan, take steps to engineer the plan in a way that creates a high probability that 90 percent or more will be invested this way. An effective strategy for accomplishing this is to periodically reenroll all your participants into the target date fund, matching their retirement date unless they opt out. While this may sound like a strategy that moves you out of your comfort zone, it's a growing trend you should consider.

In 2016, Vanguard examined the impact of a reenrollment event within a large defined contribution plan.[21] They analyzed participant behavior immediately after the event, after six months, and after one year. Six months after reenrollment, they found 94 percent of participants and 74 percent of plan assets were still in target date funds. One year later, 92 percent of participants and 81 percent of plan assets were in TDFs.

Further, in our employee survey, we found that 61 percent of respondents viewed TDF reenrollment favorably.

Communicated effectively, reenrollment is an effective strategy that is well received by participants. For most people, it's a nonissue, especially when presented with the rationale behind it. Furthermore, anyone who wishes to be excluded can opt out.

CHAPTER 9

Implementing an Automatic Features Strategy (Pd)

Now that I've walked you through the compelling evidence and research for automatic plan design, let me highlight how to bring it all together. The key to the successful adoption of an automatic features program that gets your participants on the path to retirement success depends on implementation.

Start with a minimum default rate of 6 percent, an annual escalation rate of at least 1 percent up to a cap of 15 to 20 percent, and periodically reenrolling participants into a Qualified Default Investment Alternative (QDIA), such as a target date fund (TDF). Remember that they can always opt out, but most won't.

One of the most important decisions you will need to make is whether to add these automatic features for new hires only or existing employees, too. I recommend automatically enrolling eligible employees who are not currently participating in the plan.

This is known as retroactive automatic enrollment. I also recommend increasing anyone saving below the default percentage up to the default. For instance, if your plan's default is 6 percent, anyone saving between 1 percent and 5 percent should be increased to 6 percent, unless they opt out. At Greenspring Advisors, we call this an undersaver sweep. This approach encourages active decision-making each year and provides an important nudge for those who intend to join but have difficulty overcoming their own inertia or forgetfulness.

These approaches are very effective for participants who fail to take action on their own. But there's also a better way to help participants who do take the initiative to enroll through a streamlined process. This is accomplished by creating "curated" options to choose from, much like a prix fixe menu at a restaurant.

With the advancement of mobile technology, many larger record-keepers have made the enrollment process as simple as three clicks. First, an enrollment screen is presented, and the new participant can choose to enroll at one of three levels, such as 8 percent, 10 percent, or 12 percent. Next, they are presented with an escalation screen with the default choice of 1 percent or 2 percent. Finally, they are presented with the TDF option that corresponds to their age and projected retirement date.

All the curated options are chosen by the plan sponsor, and the employee can always override the system and choose a different option (e.g., enrolling at 11 percent). But most employees will simply progress through each screen and select from the options that are shown to them. This is a particularly effective strategy to increase deferral rates if the options are chosen wisely.

As I previously mentioned, one downside to automatic enrollment is that it can cause average deferral rates to go down when the default is set too low. Research has shown that people who enroll on their own tend to select higher deferral percentages than when automatically enrolled.

By presenting actively enrolled participants with three options to choose from that are higher than the default rate, you can almost guarantee they will enter the plan at a much higher percentage. Interestingly, this is true no matter what percentages are presented because people have all sorts of cognitive biases that impact how they make decisions, often negatively.

Traditional economics assumes that people rationally analyze all factors before they make decisions or determine the value of something. It's certainly an elegant idea, but in the real world, the decision-making process is rarely that simple.

In his fascinating book *Predictably Irrational*, Dan Ariely references a *New York Times* story about a restaurant consultant named Gregg Rapp who helps design pricing for menus. "One thing Rapp has learned is that high-priced entrees on the menu boost revenue for the restaurant—even if no one buys them," Ariely writes.

> Why? Because even though people generally won't buy the most expensive dish on the menu, they will order the second most expensive dish. Thus, by creating an expensive dish, a restauranteur can lure customers into ordering the second most expensive choice (which can be cleverly engineered to deliver a higher profit margin).

Decisions are almost never made on an absolute basis. Everything is relative and based on the options that are available.

In behavioral economics, there's a concept known as the center-stage effect. There's a lot of research that shows when people are presented with multiple options that are similar, most will choose the one in the middle. In one study, researchers found that given a choice of three highlighters, 68 percent chose the middle one. When given a choice of three chairs, 71 percent chose the middle seat.[22] When examining people's preference for choosing the middle option, Ariely describes this as "landing your plane between the runway lights."

Marketers use this technique all the time on the internet. A product or service will provide three options (e.g., basic, premium, and premier), and there's usually a "best value" icon by the middle option.

So what do relativity, restaurant menus, and the center-stage effect have to do with curating enrollment percentages? A lot, actually. If you set the options at 8, 10, and 12 percent, there's a strong likelihood that a majority of people will enroll at 10 percent, choosing the middle option and avoiding the "high-priced" choice (i.e., 12 percent).

The key is that they are choosing between the options presented, not percentages that are not shown. By choosing 10 percent, they are enrolling at a much higher percentage than the default and moving much closer (and faster) to the types of savings rate required for a successful retirement.

But what if you increase the available options to 10 percent, 12 percent, and 14 percent? I suspect you would see the majority of people choose 12 percent because of the relativity factor. When choosing these types of curated options, I'd strongly encourage you to be aggressive. Remember, participants can always choose to override the system (but they probably won't).

We explored compelling evidence in the last chapter that showed most participants fare better in professionally managed portfolios. With that in mind, you should periodically reenroll anyone into the default option that hasn't used it properly (i.e., investing 100 percent of their account balance and contributions in a single option) or hasn't made investment changes for more than two years. Again, this approach encourages active decision-making, and participants who wish to be excluded can always opt out.

Provider technology is rapidly evolving and gives committees and their advisors the ability to analyze data and trends on a much more granular level. If available, use these decision support tools to identify areas to take action.

Here's a step-by-step summary of an effective implementation strategy:

1. Implement automatic enrollment retroactively to target eligible employees who are not actively participating in the plan, not just new hires. This will have the most immediate impact on your plan's participation rate because a high percentage of this population will stay enrolled, getting them in the game and on the road to accumulating retirement savings.

2. Apply an undersaver sweep to any employees who are participating in the plan but saving at a rate below the default percentage. For instance, if your plan's default percentage is 6 percent, anyone saving between 1 and 5 percent should be increased to 6 percent, unless they opt out.

3. Escalate anyone saving at the current default or higher each year until they hit the escalation cap, which you should set at 15 to 20 percent.

4. Create streamlined enrollment solutions with curated options,

making sure to set the enrollment percentages at an appropriately high level.

5. Implement these plan design strategies on an annual or biannual basis to help encourage the right savings behaviors and help people who are stuck. Often, your employees may change their minds or wish to participate, but their inertia gets in the way. Periodic implementation avoids the risk of employees making a one-time election and being forgotten or left behind.

6. Implement a QDIA reenrollment every couple of years to help ensure that employees are properly diversified.

CASE STUDY

In 2015, we were hired by a large law firm. Prior to hiring us, the plan did not use automatic enrollment or automatic escalation and had a participation rate of 67 percent in 2014 for staff and associates (approximately 1,200 participants).

We convinced the committee to implement both those features for staff and associates, using a default rate of 6 percent and annual escalation of 1 percent up to a cap of 12 percent. The committee also agreed to automatically enroll eligible, nonparticipating employees and boost participating employees, saving less than the default up to 6 percent. Anyone at 6 percent was then escalated by 1 percent each year.

Based on our advice, the committee also took an aggressive approach, implementing these strategies each year to great success. By the end of 2018, the participation rate for these two populations jumped all the way to 89 percent!

2

Pd

Plan Design

SUMMARY

- In Hal Hershfield's social science study, survey participants who saw their future selves saved twice as much money for retirement as participants who saw their current selves ($172 versus $80).
- In Dr. Lee and De Santis's analysis, waiting to save for five years (age thirty instead of twenty-five) required annual savings increases of nearly 3 percent, and waiting ten years required a 7-percent-per-year increase.
- According to PLANSPONSOR, approximately 48 percent of plans use automatic enrollment, and 23 percent use automatic escalation.
- According to Fidelity, in the third quarter of 2019, the average participation rate for automatic enrollment plans was 88.3 percent versus 52.3 percent for voluntary enrollment plans.
- Vanguard found that participation rates for employees earning $15,000 to $30,000 a year increased from 38 percent in voluntary enrollment plans to 88 percent for automatic enrollment

plans. For those under twenty-five, the participation rate increased from 18 percent to 82 percent.

- T. Rowe Price has seen the percentage of plans with a 6 percent default increase from 18.7 percent in 2012 to 36.9 percent in 2018.

- In 2010, a joint study by EBRI and DCIIA found that simply setting the automatic escalation cap at 15 percent increased the probability of achieving an 80 percent replacement rate by 16.4 percent for the lowest-income workers and 14.1 percent for the highest-income workers.

- In a 2016 impact study of a reenrollment event by a large defined contribution plan, Vanguard found that 92 percent of participants and 81 percent of plan assets were still in TDFs after one year.

- Implement automatic enrollment for new hires and retroactively for any eligible nonparticipating employees and use a minimum 6 percent default percentage.

- Use automatic escalation of 1 to 2 percent and increase to a cap of at least 15 percent.

- Create curated enrollment menus.

- Use an undersaver sweep to target and increase any currently participating employees who are saving below the default percentage.

- Implement these changes on an annual or biannual basis.

- Implement a QDIA reenrollment every couple of years.

1. Does your plan use automatic enrollment?
2. Is your default percentage at least 6 percent?
3. Do you sweep nonparticipating employees and undersavers into the plan?
4. Does your plan use automatic escalation of at least 1 percent?
5. Is your escalation cap at least 15 percent?
6. Have you done a QDIA reenrollment?

3

Fs

Fee Structure

CHAPTER 10

─────

The Evolution of the Fee Landscape (Fs)

When I was a kid in the 1980s, I loved to watch cartoons. One of my favorites was *G.I. Joe*. At the end of each episode, there was a short public service announcement (PSA) that was meant to teach kids life lessons so they could make good decisions.

For instance, there would be a situation where a group of children would be faced with a tough choice (e.g., telling the truth, not getting in a car with a stranger, etc.). Then Duke, Lady Jaye, Snake Eyes, or another character would appear and provide guidance and counsel to them. Each PSA ended with the kid saying, "Now I know," and the *G.I. Joe* character saying, "Because knowing is half the battle!"

If you make key decisions about your organization's retirement plan, then you have a huge responsibility to your employees and to your organization under the law. The difficulty lies in how hard it is to know what to do, much less do it.

Knowing what steps to take in order to control the fees your plan and participants pay is an area of significant importance, both from a legal standpoint and in terms of long-term outcomes for your people. It's also an area that has come under intense scrutiny from a legal and regulatory perspective in the media and in the minds of American workers. But even in the current era of "fee disclosure," it's difficult for plan decision-makers to get a clear picture and make smarter financial decisions. A sampling of the comments I hear include:

- "I have no idea what we are paying in fees."
- "I am concerned our fees are too high, but I don't have a way of knowing for sure."
- "I am worried about my fiduciary risk because I keep reading about lawsuits."
- "I'm too busy to worry about fees, and it's not my money anyway."

In the twelve years since I first wrote extensively about retirement plan fees in *Fixing the 401(k)* and helped spur the industry on to greater levels of transparency, the fee landscape has changed dramatically, shaped primarily by four driving forces.

First, the DOL implemented two different fee disclosure regulations aimed at creating additional transparency for both plan sponsors and participants. The 408(b)(2) regulation (i.e., "Plan Sponsor Disclosure") and the 404(a)(5) (i.e., "Participant Disclosure") both went into effect in 2012.

Regulation 408(b)(2) requires that covered service providers (e.g., brokers, advisors, recordkeepers, TPAs, etc.) provide fiduciaries of ERISA plans with a description of the services they provide, the compensation they expect to receive in connection with those services, and which services (if any) they provide on a fiduciary basis. The purpose of 408(b)(2) is to put plan fiduciaries (e.g., committee members) in a better position to understand fees and compensation so they can make prudent decisions.

Using the information disclosed under 408(b)(2), 404(a)(5) requires that plan sponsors of participant-directed ERISA plans provide certain information to plan participants, including the disclosure of fees, expenses, and other plan and investment-related information. The purpose of 404(a)(5) is to create greater transparency and give participants a better understanding of the fees and expenses associated with their account.

In the real world, while these disclosures created conversations, they did little to foster any real understanding by either intended audience. Let me give a quick example. In 2012, not long after the disclosure rules went into effect, I had lunch with the former controller of a prospect who is now one of my best clients. The company had been using a well-known broker in the area for a long time, but they were looking to make a change. The controller explained that one reason was an overall lack of fee transparency: "I have no idea how much we are paying in fees," he said. "I have the sense we are getting screwed. I just can't prove it."

He then handed me the 408(b)(2) disclosure he had recently received. I took a pen and began circling different fees on the page, explaining what the numbers meant, what services they were for, and who was receiving them. After five minutes, he had a complete picture of the situation and hired our firm, primarily because of that single conversation.

I learned two important things that day. First, with government regulations, it's possible to be compliant and still confused. Second, disclosure without context is meaningless. What's ironic is that the service providers on the plan had complied with the regulations, but the broker had failed to explain the information to the client in a simple, clear way. The broker thought he'd done his job by providing the information and checked that box. However, he didn't get credit for it (and lost the engagement) because the client didn't realize he already had the information.

Second, the litigation environment has shined a spotlight on the risks associated with excessive fees and breaches of fiduciary duty. Many *Fortune* 1000 companies and well-known institutions of higher education have agreed to multimillion-dollar settlements due to excessive fee claims. In particular, the efforts and work of a single law firm in Saint Louis (Schlichter Bogard & Denton) who pioneered 401(k) excessive fee litigation beginning in 2006 has had an incredible impact on the industry, bringing awareness to fees and the importance of fiduciary responsibility in a major way. Jerry Schlichter has been referred to as the "Lone Ranger of the 401(k)s"[23] and "public enemy no. 1 for 401(k) profiteers,"[24] a man whose name brings fear to plan fiduciaries far and wide. Personally, I agree with many of his perspectives, and I appreciate the attention and awareness his efforts have created. Litigation has made it easier to convince clients to make changes because you can point back to case law as a reference point.

Third, the media has played a role. I think the single most significant piece of media coverage about 401(k) fees and fiduciary responsibility was by John Oliver on his HBO show *Last Week Tonight*. Oliver famously takes on various industries and exposes questionable business practices. If you're the subject of one of his segments, you're in trouble. In 2016, Oliver looked at the impact of high fees and what he learned after he asked his production company to set up a 401(k) plan using a well-known recordkeeper for his employees.[25] If you haven't seen the video, do yourself a favor and watch it. It's hysterical, enlightening, and embarrassing for the retirement industry. In the weeks after this episode aired, I had more people ask me if I was a fiduciary than ever before.

Finally, fiduciary advisors that specialize in working with corporate retirement plans have made fees a front-and-center issue by creating a context-based approach to understanding, benchmarking, and negotiating more efficient fee arrangements.

CHAPTER 11

Litigation Trends (Fs)

For those of you keeping score at home, the pace of 401(k) and 403(b) fee litigation is increasing. Many large companies are being sued. Even institutions of higher education are in the crosshairs. I recently did a Google search for "401(k) litigation" that returned nearly 1.4 million results!

According to a 2018 report by the Center for Retirement Research at Boston College, there were eight 401(k) complaints filed in 2006, eighteen in 2007, and a peak of 107 in 2008.[26] This number declined over the next five years, bottoming out in 2013, with only two new complaints. However, in 2016 and 2017, there were more than one hundred new complaints filed. The researchers found that of the roughly 430 cases they evaluated, 60 percent were still pending, 20 percent were dismissed or closed, 16 percent were settled or decided, and 4 percent were still on appeal.

As I mentioned in the last chapter, when these lawsuits first became popular, it was primarily Jerry Schlichter who pioneered these cases and developed the playbook on how to litigate from a plaintiff's standpoint. For instance, his bio page states that "he and the firm have obtained settlements in these 401(k) excessive fee cases of more than $300 million for employees and retirees."[27] They have also obtained the three largest 401(k) excessive fee settlements in history—a $62 million settlement against Lockheed Martin, a $57 million settlement against Boeing, and a $55 million settlement from ABB, Inc. Each one of these cases also included nonmonetary compensation. The attorneys' fees in these three cases equated to roughly 30 percent, so close to $55 million!

Attracted by these types of large settlements, more plaintiff's attorneys are getting into the mix. The primary goal in each case seems to be the same: get past the motion to dismiss phase and force the defendant into a very expensive discovery process, incentivizing large settlements.

As an example, an industry colleague recently told me he received a voicemail from a gentleman "seeking an expert in the standards of care regarding appointing and monitoring fiduciaries for 401(k) plans." Turns out he's recruiting expert witnesses for a law firm.

The common complaints in these cases have been about excessive fees being charged, imprudent selection of share classes, inappropriate investment options being offered to participants, and alleged conflicts of interest between plans and their service providers.

ERISA does not spell out the types of investment options that are appropriate, what levels of fees are reasonable, or how to monitor either of these. Instead, ERISA requires that fiduciaries show "the care, skill, prudence, and diligence…that a prudent man" would when choosing investments "so as to minimize the risk of large losses" and "defray reasonable expenses of administering the plan."[28] The language in ERISA makes it clear that what matters most is the process, not the outcome. Where a settlement was obtained, it was argued that fiduciaries either didn't engage in a prudent process or hadn't consistently implemented one.

Here is a list of some of the most high-profile excessive fee settlements:

401(K)

- Lockheed Martin—$62 million
- Boeing—$57 million
- ABB—$55 million
- Cigna—$35 million
- International Paper—$30 million
- Anthem—$23.65 million
- American Airlines—$22 million
- Philips North America—$17 million
- Caterpillar—$16.5 million
- Walmart—$13.5 million
- Edison International—$13.2 million
- Safeway—$8.5 million
- JCPenney—$4.5 million

403(B)

- MIT—$18.1 million
- Duke—$10.65 million
- Vanderbilt—$14.5 million
- Johns Hopkins—$14 million
- University of Chicago—$6.5 million
- Brown—$3.5 million

In one of the more ironic twists over the past few years, guess which industry has been a source of targets? The retirement industry! Here's a list of settlements for excessive fees against financial services companies *by their own employees*:

- Ameriprise—$27.5 million
- BB&T—$24 million
- Deutsche Bank—$21.9 million
- Franklin Templeton—$14 million
- Fidelity—$12 million
- Allianz—$12 million
- Waddell & Reed—$4.9 million
- Jackson National—$4.5 million
- Transamerica—$3.8 million
- Edward Jones—$3.2 million
- New York Life—settled for $3 million

Amazingly, it appears these companies providing services to corporate retirement plans can't even properly oversee *their own* 401(k) plans for *their own* employees. Talk about a case of the cobbler's children having no shoes! Of course, the companies that have settled don't admit wrongdoing, and many others that have pending litigation will still have their day in court to defend themselves against allegations.

As someone who has worked as a retirement fiduciary for almost fifteen years, I can tell you I am not surprised by this at all. What is surprising to me is that many plan sponsors think these vendors have their best interests in mind when they are not held to fiduciary standards. If you're a plan sponsor or a plan fiduciary, you've got to ask yourself, "If these service providers can't manage the fees in their own plans, how confident can I be they are helping me manage the fees in my plan?"

This is why I believe the role of a fiduciary advisor is so critical to effective plan governance and why most companies are turning to 401(k) and 403(b) specialists. A specialist advisor with the right experience as an ERISA fiduciary, a commitment to fiduciary principles and practices, and the courage and conviction to hold vendors accountable is essential to protecting the interests of participants and keeping companies out of hot water.

As I also mentioned, these settlements commonly include nonmonetary relief as well. These are instructive because they highlight best practices. For instance, in *David B. Tracey et al. v. Massachusetts Institute of Technology et al.*, MIT agreed that for a three-year period, it would:

- Provide annual training to plan fiduciaries on prudent and loyal practices under ERISA and proper decision-making in the exclusive best interests of plan participants.
- Issue request for proposals from at least three qualified service providers for recordkeeping and administrative services for the plan.
- Ensure fees for the recordkeeper are not billed as a percentage of assets but on a flat-fee-per-participant model.
- Ensure any revenue sharing related to plan investments not used to defray lawful plan expenses would be deposited in the plan trust and be returned to plan participants at least annually.

In the next few chapters, I'll teach you how to better understand plan economics and take steps to avoid the risk of litigation.

CHAPTER 12

Assessing the Risks (Fs)

WHAT ARE THE RISKS TO YOUR COMPANY?

Okay, so you get the picture. Large organizations are getting sued (and often losing/settling) because of fee mismanagement. Meanwhile, the pace of litigation is increasing. Here's a key point to keep in mind: big companies are losing lawsuits despite having large, sophisticated HR and finance teams that you'd think would be knowledgeable and effective in this area. But if they have been making major mistakes, what's the likelihood a small company is doing a better job without the same resources?

Let me state that I think the industry overhypes risk of fee litigation, especially for smaller plans, even though there have been a couple of instances where these types of plans have been targeted. I call this fiduciary fearmongering. While it's possible for plans of any size to be sued, it's not probable, and as long as you take the right steps, the risk of litigation is likely to be very low. Consider driving a car. Whenever I drive, I'm always at risk of an accident. But if I drive safely and obey traffic laws, the possibility that I'll be involved in a serious crash is reduced by a wide margin.

Throughout the next four chapters, I will teach you a handful of simple, practical steps that can drastically reduce your possibility of losing a fee lawsuit. However, the threat of litigation isn't the only risk companies face if they don't negotiate wisely. A second risk for companies is related to human capital and talent management. That's because it's the employees who bear the brunt of high fees when plan sponsors contribute little direct cost. Unhappy, dissatisfied employees have both a direct and indirect cost on company culture and company performance.

Most companies pay little attention to retirement plan fees for three main reasons.

First, most fiduciaries don't realize the significance of their legal responsibilities under ERISA. In many cases, they may not even know that they are fiduciaries. For example, a 2014 survey by AllianceBernstein found that 37 percent of the 1,000 plan sponsors surveyed were unaware of their fiduciary status, and 6 percent were unsure.[29] Here's the catch: every single person surveyed was actually a fiduciary!

Second, they don't see most fees because they never hit the company's bottom line, so there's little incentive to reduce costs. In my experience, more than 95 percent of fees are paid through the plan.

And third, they aren't aware of the devastating impact fees can have on long-term retirement savings.

The DOL has made it clear that companies have an ongoing legal obligation to understand and evaluate plan fees to help their employees achieve a secure financial future. In "Understanding Retirement Plan Fees and Expenses," the DOL states:

Understanding and evaluating plan fees and expenses associated with plan investments, investment options, and services are an important part of a fiduciary's responsibility. This responsibility is ongoing. After careful evaluation during the initial selection, you will want to monitor plan fees and expenses to determine whether they continue to be reasonable in light of the services provided.[30]

A failure to understand, monitor, and control fees put plan sponsors at risk for legal action by employees for potential breach of fiduciary duty.

WHAT ARE THE RISKS TO YOUR EMPLOYEES?

There are four primary variables that contribute to the retirement equation.

First, the total amount of money that goes into a person's account, including their own contributions plus any employer contributions. Studies have shown that this is the most important variable, and most experts recommend total savings rates of 10 to 20 percent depending on age and income level. Second, the total amount of money that comes out of their account, like fees, loans, cash-outs, hardship withdrawals, etc. Third, the rate of return they earn on their investments. Most people think this is the most important driver of retirement security, but it's not, and it's also the one people have the least control over. Furthermore, a person can't invest their way out of a savings deficit, which is why sufficient funding is so important. The last variable is time. The earlier someone saves, the lower their long-term savings rates typically need to be and the higher the probability of achieving a successful retirement experience. As we've seen, delaying retirement saving by even five to ten years can have a devastating impact.

For this chapter, let's focus on how high fees can impact that equation. The DOL has estimated that high retirement fees can reduce a person's account balance by 28 percent over the course of a working career.[31] Let's assume you began your career at twenty-five and made a starting salary of $40,000, receiving an annual pay raise of 3 percent. Let's also assume you saved diligently and contributed 10 percent of your salary to your 401(k) plan each year and received a 3 percent matching contribution from your employer for a total annual savings rate of 13 percent. Finally, you earned an average annual return of 7 percent on your investments after fees. Guess how much you would have retired with at age sixty-five? About $1.8 million. Now imagine you worked for a company that had a 401(k) plan with expenses that were 0.50 percent higher, reducing your after-fee returns to 6.5 percent. Instead of retiring with approximately $1.8 million, you retire with about $1.6 million (11 percent less) because high fees were eating away at your balance year after year. Want to know how much additional income you could have had for the rest of your life with that $200,000? $1,022 *per month.*[32] Ouch!

What could one of your employees do with an additional $1,000 per month in income? How much would that impact their living situation, their ability to pay for healthcare expenses, how often they could see their grandchildren, or the chance to leave a legacy to organizations they care about? That $1,000 in monthly income could be the difference between retiring in dignity or with despair. It also could have systemic implications. What if that $1,000 per month could have been the difference between being financially independent and being a financial burden to their family? What if they had to move in with their children, or they had to pay for their long-term care, which meant they couldn't save enough for retirement, and the cycle continued to their children and their children's children?

Low fees alone will not save your employees' retirement prospects, but they can have a significant impact and help them keep a lot more of what they save. However, your employees have very little control over the fees they pay because they don't select the vendors that service the plan, the investments that are offered, or the overall fee structure. As I've established, those things are all chosen by the plan fiduciaries. That means your employees are highly dependent on you to make wise decisions.

QUANTIFYING THE IMPACT FROM A CORPORATE FINANCE PERSPECTIVE

It's in the best interest of companies to gain control of retirement plan fees, both to manage corporate risk and also to engender employee goodwill. I've already quantified the estimated financial impact on employees. But since most plan fees aren't paid by the company, reducing costs isn't often seen as high a priority from a corporate finance perspective because it doesn't affect the bottom line. The best way for companies to get motivated is to quantify the long-term impact of high fees, at both the plan level and at the employee level.

Most CFOs can create a present value (PV) formula in Excel in their sleep. So that's a great place to start. Think of retirement plan fees like any other potential business expense, even though very little direct cost may hit the company's P&L statement. Just in case you slept through your finance class in college, let me refresh your memory about present value. Present value is what a future sum of money or a stream of cash flow is worth in today's dollars. You determine present value by taking a future sum of money and then using an interest rate (called the discount rate) to factor in the time value of money. The higher the discount rate, the lower the present value of that future sum of money.

At a plan level, one way to think about the long-term impact of high fees is to project the impact over a period of time (e.g., ten years). So put on your CFO hat. Let's assume you have a $20 million 401(k) plan with 200 participants, and the current total annual fees equate to 0.80 percent of plan assets ($160,000/year). Also, let's assume that participants pay all plan fees, so there is no direct cost to your company.

If the plan grows at 5 percent over the next ten years (for simplicity, I will assume this includes market growth plus annual contributions, such as employee deferrals and employer contributions), there will be roughly $31 million in the plan. With annual plan fees of 0.80 percent remaining constant over that period, the cumulative fees paid would be $2,013,601.

However, consider if you had negotiated plan fees of 0.40 percent during that same ten-year period. The plan would have only paid $1,029,394 in fees, which is a difference of $984,207! Look at this chart to see the difference:

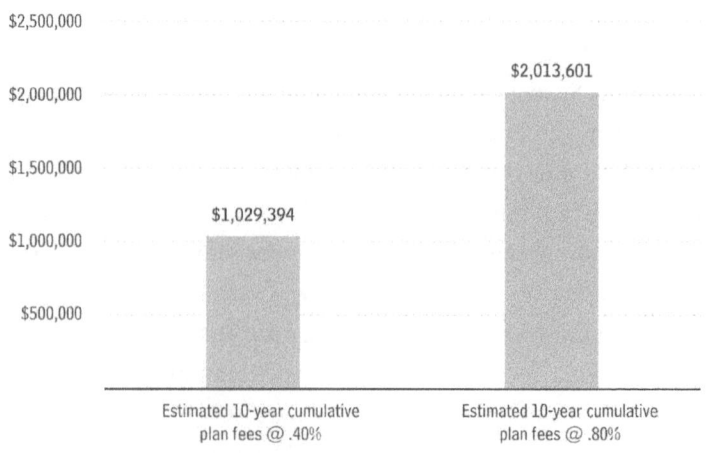

10 Year Cumulative Plan Fees

Now, using a discount rate of 4 percent, the present value of that $984,207 in additional fees is worth $664,895 in today's dollars, which is like depositing that amount of money in the plan today. With 200 participants, that's like giving each one of them $3,324 in additional retirement assets ($664,895 ÷ 200) just from fee savings!

Remember that you're still wearing your CFO hat. If you were projected to spend more than $2 million on IT services over the next decade and someone told you they could save you nearly $700,000 in today's dollars, would you listen? I expect you would jump at the chance to save this kind of money for your company (otherwise, you may not be CFO for long)! The difference is that the cost of IT is a direct expense that hits the bottom line of your company's P&L, while retirement plan fees do not since they are paid through the plan and absorbed by your employees. Because of a lack of awareness, a lack of concern, or both, companies rarely have the same level of commitment to reducing plan costs. From a fiduciary perspective (and for the good of your employees' financial futures), that kind of thinking needs to change. This example illustrates the importance of thinking about retirement plan fees like any other corporate expense and applying a similar decision-making logic to the process.

═══

CHAPTER 13

Understanding Plan Economics (Fs)

Retirement plan economics can be confusing and complex. In this chapter, I will show you which factors drive plan pricing so you can use this knowledge to your advantage.

First, you need to get a clear picture of all the potential hands in the cookie jar. Who are the different service providers in the industry, and what are their different roles and responsibilities? Once you know the service providers you need for your plan, you can assess which services are necessary and worth paying for and which ones are superfluous and unnecessary.

Here's a high-level overview of the most common service providers and a basic description of their roles, responsibilities, fiduciary capacity, and the potential for conflicts of interest.

Role	Responsibilities	Fiduciary Status	Potential for Conflicts
Recordkeeper	Manages day-to-day operations, like processing enrollments, managing and tracking employee investments, implementing automatic features, and processing and tracking any contributions and distributions (e.g., pretax contributions, Roth, employer pretax match, rollovers, loans, hardship withdrawals, etc.). The recordkeeper also produces plan statements for employees and most likely provides the call center and online experience for both employees and the plan sponsor to manage and administer the plan.	No	Low, unless they have affiliated asset-management, banking, or insurance lines of business.
Third-Party Administrator (TPA)	Focuses on plan compliance, such as preparing the annual Form 5500, producing and/or managing plan documents, performing annual nondiscrimination testing, helping correct operational failures, and preparing and distributing participant notices. They may also provide plan design consulting for things like eligibility, automatic enrollment, and escalation, and analyzing profit sharing and/or matching scenarios.	No, unless providing 3(16) services	Low
Registered Investment Adviser (RIA)	Provide services to the plan and/or participants to assist with fiduciary governance, investment selection and monitoring, investment advice, plan benchmarking, fee analysis, vendor selection, compliance support, plan design consulting, employee engagement, etc. Investment-related services are provided as an ERISA 3(21) or ERISA 3(38) fiduciary.	Yes	Low
Broker or "Registered Representative"	May be similar to the services offered by an RIA but on a nonfiduciary basis.	No	High

Role	Responsibilities	Fiduciary Status	Potential for Conflicts
Directed Trustee	Holds plan assets but does not control them—they serve in a very limited fiduciary capacity and are subject to the direction of a named fiduciary in accordance with the terms of the plan document and ERISA.	Typically, but limited	Low
Custodian	Similar to a directed trustee—they act as an agent of the plan (but not as a fiduciary) and hold plan assets but lack any discretionary authority with respect to those assets and take direction from a named trustee.	No	Low
Asset Managers	Mutual fund and/or investment companies manage the actual investment vehicles in the plan (e.g., mutual funds or collective investment trusts [CITs]). They provide portfolio management services and buy and sell the underlying securities within the investment vehicles.	No	Low, unless they have affiliated recordkeeping, banking, or insurance lines of business.

WHAT DRIVES PLAN PRICING

Administrative pricing (e.g., recordkeeping, administration, discrimination testing, Form 5500 preparation, etc.) for a retirement plan is driven by the following factors:

1. **Total assets**—How much money is in the plan across all account balances.
2. **Total participants with a balance**—How many active and terminated employees have balances in the plan.
3. **Average account balance**—The total assets divided by total participants with a balance.
4. **Net cash flows**—The total amount of money contributed to the plan each year (in the form of employee deferrals and employer contributions, like a match, profit sharing, etc.).

Plans with a high average account balance (total assets ÷ total participants with a balance) and strong cash flow tend to get the lowest pricing. For example, let's compare two plans with the same assets. Plan A has $10 million in assets and 100 participants for an average account balance of $100,000. Plan B also has $10 million in assets but 500 participants for an average account balance of $20,000. I would expect Plan B to be priced higher because it has five times the number of participants, which means more statements, more calls into the phone center, a larger population for discrimination testing purposes, and so on.

In most cases, advisor pricing tends to be tied to the size of assets. Therefore, a $20 million plan would expect to pay a higher fee than a $5 million plan. However, advisory fees compress and level off around $50 million in plan assets. A $100 million plan rarely pays a significantly higher advisory fee than a $50 million plan for a comparable scope of services.

UNDERSTANDING FEE STRUCTURES

There are five basic fee structures within the industry:

1. **Asset-based**—Fees are charged as a percentage of assets (e.g., 0.25 percent).
2. **Fixed**—Fees are charged as a flat dollar amount (e.g., $25,000).
3. **Per participant**—Fees are charged by participant (e.g., $75/ participant).
4. **Revenue sharing**—Fees are offset using a portion of the investment fees (e.g., 12b-1 fees of 0.50 percent).
5. **Transactional**—Fees are event-driven (e.g., $100 to take a loan or withdrawal).

Many plans are still tied to some sort of asset-based pricing model.

This is by far the most common approach, and the industry likes this model because it means that as plan assets grow, fees also increase.

PAYMENT SOURCES

There are only two sources of payment for plan fees:

1. **Company**—Fees paid directly or indirectly by the plan sponsor as a billable expense.
2. **Participants**—Fees paid by participants either directly through their individual accounts or indirectly through the investments they select.

Each source can pay expenses directly. For instance, a company could hire an advisor and pay its annual advisory fee of $40,000 directly from corporate assets. The fiduciaries could also elect to pay that fee through the plan, and participants would pay a portion of that fee each year directly from their accounts.

Two indirect sources of payment are:

1. Forfeitures
2. Revenue sharing

Paying fees from forfeitures is technically a company expense. Forfeitures occur when a participant leaves the company before their employer contributions (e.g., matching or profit sharing) are fully vested. For instance, if a terminated participant has $25,000 in total employer contributions but is only 50 percent vested, they will forfeit $12,500. This amount goes into the plan's forfeiture account, and the plan sponsor has the choice to offset future employer contributions or current administrative fees.

For example, if the company had to make matching contributions of $100,000, they could use the $12,500 to offset that $100,000 and then only fund the remaining $87,500. Alternatively, the company could use the $12,500 to pay plan expenses. In the previous example, they could use the $12,500 to pay a portion of the $40,000 advisory fee and then pay the remaining $27,500 from the company. In that case, the company would then have to make the full $100,000 matching contribution for the year because there would be no forfeitures left. Forfeitures cannot be refunded to the company because they are considered a plan asset, but forfeitures can offset the direct cost of the plan for certain expenses.

METHODS OF ALLOCATION

Once you have determined which types and amounts of fees are appropriate, you need to decide how to allocate these fees. According to leading ERISA attorney Fred Reish, the method of fee allocation is a fiduciary decision that, in his experience, many fiduciaries fail to handle prudently.[33]

There are two primary methods of allocating fees:

1. **Pro rata**—Fees are allocated on a prorated basis determined by a participant's account balance as it relates to other balances in the plan.
2. **Per capita**—Fees are allocated on a per-participant basis.

To illustrate the difference, let's consider the impact on account balances for a recordkeeping fee of 0.20 percent (pro rata) versus $100 per participant (per capita):

PRO RATA

Balance	Recordkeeping Fee (%)	Recordkeeping Fee ($)
$10,000	0.20%	$20
$25,000	0.20%	$50
$50,000	0.20%	$100
$100,000	0.20%	$200
$250,000	0.20%	$500

PER CAPITA

Balance	Recordkeeping Fee (%)	Recordkeeping Fee ($)
$10,000	1.00%	$100
$25,000	0.40%	$100
$50,000	0.20%	$100
$100,000	0.10%	$100
$250,000	0.04%	$100

As you can see, pro rata fees benefit smaller balance participants because the fees are in relation to the size of their account balance. In the first example, every participant in the plan pays 0.20 percent for recordkeeping services. So a participant with a $10,000 account balance would pay $20 per year with the pro rata method, while the participant with a balance ten times larger ($100,000) would pay $200 per year for the same services. In contrast, per capita fees benefit larger balance employees and are better for participants over time because these fees decrease as a percentage of assets as balances grow. In the second example, every participant in the plan pays $100 for recordkeeping services, regardless of their account balance. This means that a participant with a $10,000 account balance would pay 1 percent per year on a percentage basis with the per capita method, while the participant with the ten times larger balance ($100,000) would pay 0.10 percent per year for the same services.

From a fiduciary perspective, the allocation decision is important. The DOL has provided guidance that the pro rata method is equitable in most cases, while the per capita method may be reasonable, although the fiduciary "has considerable discretion in determining the method of expense allocation."[34]

A simple way to analyze the allocation decision that I've developed is to build a spreadsheet with two tabs that include every participant's account balance. On the first tab, you create a fixed-fee formula and on the second tab, an asset-based formula to determine how much each participant would pay in both dollars and as a percentage of assets. You also determine the break-even account balance where participants would benefit from fixed fees as compared to asset-based fees. Using this information, you can analyze which method would benefit the highest percentage of participants.

For instance, in a plan with a lot of younger employees or a lot of new hires (with lower account balances), it may make sense to apply fees pro rata. However, if a plan has a lot of high-balance participants, it may be more beneficial to allocate some fees on a per capita basis. This is one of those decisions that can vary from plan to plan based on demographics. There's no one-size-fits-all method.

CHAPTER 14

Revenue Sharing and Conflicts of Interest (Fs)

REVENUE SHARING AND SHARE CLASSES

A major focus of excessive fee litigation has been the argument that fiduciary breaches have arisen for imprudent share class selection and improper usage of revenue sharing. I'd like to discuss some of the challenges and complexities associated with both.

Every mutual fund has fees deducted at the fund level before returns are calculated. These fees are known as expense ratios and cover the costs to manage the investment option (i.e., investment management, operations, and legal expenses). A portion of the expense ratio can include revenue sharing, which may offset some or all of the plan's administrative expenses. Recordkeepers, TPAs, and advisors/brokers may receive revenue sharing payments from some or all mutual funds in a plan to help pay for each respective service provided to the plan. This is called indirect compensation because it comes from the funds instead of directly from the plan or participant accounts.

Many mutual funds have various share classes that are identically managed but have different fee structures associated with them, including different amounts of revenue sharing, which go by names such as 12b-1, subtransfer agency, or administrative services fees. Think of share classes as different trim levels of the same make and model of a car. For instance, I own a Ram 1500 pickup truck, which comes in six different versions, ranging from the least expensive (the Tradesman) to the most expensive (the Limited). When buying a vehicle, the highest trim level has the most features and luxury items and costs the most. You pay more, but you get more. With mutual funds, it's the inverse—the more you pay, the less you get because those fees reduce your net returns. When buying a mutual fund, you want to purchase the least expensive share class because that will deliver the highest net return. Here's an example of the six different retirement share classes for the American Funds Growth Fund of America, including the expense ratio and revenue sharing amounts:[35]

Ticker	Share Class	Management Fee	12b-1 Fee	Sub-TA Fee	Other Fees	Total Expense Ratio	2018 Return*
RGAAX	R-1	0.27%	1.00%	0.10%	0.04%	1.41%	−3.66%
RGABX	R-2	0.27%	0.75%	0.25%	0.14%	1.41%	−3.67%
RGACX	R-3	0.27%	0.50%	0.15%	0.04%	0.96%	−3.25%
RGAEX	R-4	0.27%	0.25%	0.10%	0.04%	0.66%	−2.95%
RGAFX	R-5	0.27%	0.00%	0.05%	0.04%	0.36%	−2.66%
RGAGX	R-6	0.27%	0.00%	0.00%	0.04%	0.31%	−2.60%

*Returns provided by Morningstar.

There are some important things to note. First, the total expense ratio *equals* the sum of the management fee, 12b-1 fee, Sub-TA fee, and other fees. Second, the management fee goes to American Funds as compensation for managing the fund, and the amount (0.27 percent) is uniform across every share class. Third, the "Other Fees" are uniform at 0.04 percent, except for the R-2 share class, which is slightly higher, though the math works out to the same as the R-1. Last, using the 2018 return of each share class, you can see the difference in returns is roughly the difference in total expense ratio. So what's the main difference between the share classes? It comes down to the amount of revenue sharing. Consider that 12b-1 fees are paid to brokers/advisors, while Sub-TA fees are paid to recordkeepers and TPAs, although sometimes both types of fees can be collected by the same service provider.

CONFLICTS OF INTEREST AND FEE INEQUALITY

Share classes and revenue sharing can create many issues within a plan.

First, since revenue sharing is embedded in the expense ratio of the fund, there is a natural lack of transparency. This can create confusion, mistrust, and the feeling that fees are hidden or haven't been fully disclosed. With the plan sponsor disclosures, this is a perception-versus-reality issue, like the example I used of the CFO who had the disclosure notice but didn't understand it. It's a different story, however, with participant disclosures. Here, the regulation doesn't require the actual amounts of revenue sharing to be itemized and disclosed. Rather, the participant disclosure needs only include language to the effect of "some expenses of the plan have been paid by revenue from the investment funds."

Second, the amount of revenue sharing can spiral out of control as the plan grows if plan fiduciaries aren't vigilant about monitoring share classes. For instance, let's say a plan has $1 million in it and negotiates a fee of $10,000 for a broker. The plan uses a share class that pays the broker a 12b-1 fee of 1 percent or $10,000 ($10,000 ÷ $1,000,000). Three years down the road, the plan has grown to $3 million through a combination of plan contributions, market returns, and employee growth. If the plan is still using the same share class, the broker is now receiving $30,000 in 12b-1 fees (1 percent × $3 million) or three times the amount as when they were hired. Assuming they are not providing an expanded scope of services that warrants this amount of compensation, it could be deemed excessive and imprudent. While this situation occurs a lot less than it used to, you would be surprised at how often this still happens in the real world, especially with smaller plans that don't have a strong governance process in place.

Third, the potential for conflicts of interest is high when there is revenue sharing. It's been common within plans to have some funds that revenue share and some funds that don't, which is known as "uneven" compensation. I'll illustrate my point with a simple example of a plan that has only one participant with a $100,000 account balance and only two funds in it: Fund A and Fund B. Both are large cap growth funds, except Fund A has a total expense ratio of 1 percent and a 12b-1 fee of 0.50 percent. Fund B has a total expense ratio of 0.10 percent and no 12b-1 fee. Let's assume that the nonfiduciary broker is sitting down with this participant to discuss their investments. You can see the conflict of interest and the misalignment of incentives. If the broker recommends Fund A, she will make $500 (0.50 percent × $100,000) and the participant's total portfolio expense will be $1,000 (1 percent × $100,000). But if she recommends Fund B, with no 12b-1 fee, she will earn nothing, and the participant's total portfolio expense will be $100 (0.10 percent × $100,000). Which fund is she more likely to recommend?

Another issue that uneven revenue sharing payments create is the lack of equitability or fairness for participants. That's because anyone who invests in funds that revenue share will underwrite the administrative cost for those who invest in funds that don't. This is called fee inequality.

Let's use an example of a plan with three funds (Funds A, B, and C). Fund A pays revenue sharing of 0.50 percent, Fund B pays revenue sharing of 0.25 percent, and Fund C pays no revenue sharing. Let's also assume there are three participants in the plan (Participants A, B, and C). Participants A and B both have an account balance of $100,000, and Participant C has an account balance of $50,000. Here's how the math works:

	Account Balance	Fund	Revenue Sharing Paid by the Participant in %	Administrative Fees Paid by the Participant in $
Participant A	$100,000	Fund A	0.50%	$500
Participant B	$100,000	Fund B	0.25%	$250
Participant C	$50,000	Fund C	0.00%	$0

As you can see, Participants A and B pay different administrative amounts based on the investments they choose, even though they have the same account balance. Participant C pays nothing toward the administrative cost of the plan. This creates both fee inequality and potential conflicts of interest.

Let me share four methods to solve these issues.

OPTION #1—USE THE SAME SHARE CLASS

The first method for eliminating fee inequality and conflicts of interest is to use the same share class so every fund in the plan pays the same amount in revenue sharing and also eliminates the conflict of interest. This is easier said than done. Not every fund company uses the same share class naming convention (e.g., R-3), and when they do, the amounts of revenue sharing often vary. Here's an example where all three funds pay revenue sharing of 0.50 percent, which is applied on a pro rata basis:

	Account Balance	Fund	Revenue Sharing Paid by the Participant in %	Administrative Fees Paid by the Participant in $
Participant A	$100,000	Fund A	0.50%	$500
Participant B	$100,000	Fund B	0.50%	$500
Participant C	$50,000	Fund C	0.50%	$250

Outcomes:

- Creates fee fairness and equitability.
- Lacks transparency and is difficult to communicate to participants.
- Requires the use of higher-cost share classes.
- Can be challenging to implement across multiple fund families.

OPTION #2—CREDIT REVENUE SHARING BACK TO PARTICIPANTS AND CHARGE A PRO RATA OR PER CAPITA FEE

The second method is to credit revenue sharing payments back to participants and to assess each participant a direct pro rata (%) or per capita ($) administrative fee. This also eliminates fee inequality and potential conflicts of interest. Once again, Fund A pays revenue sharing of 0.50 percent, Fund B pays revenue sharing of 0.25 percent, and Fund C pays no revenue sharing. But with this method, the revenue sharing in Fund A and Fund B is credited back to Participant A and Participant B, and all three participants are assessed a direct pro rata fee of 0.25 percent.

	Account Balance	Fund	Revenue Sharing Paid by the Participant in %	Fee Credit	Direct Pro Rata Fee	Administrative Fees Paid by the Participant in $
Participant A	$100,000	Fund A	0.50%	−0.50%	0.25%	$250
Participant B	$100,000	Fund B	0.25%	−0.25%	0.25%	$250
Participant C	$50,000	Fund C	0.00%	0.00%	0.25%	$125

Outcomes:

- Creates fee fairness and equitability.
- Makes fees more transparent.
- Can be harder to communicate to participants.
- Has additional disclosure requirements.
- Provides flexibility in allocation methods (per capita or pro rata).

OPTION #3—ADJUST REVENUE SHARING BY INVESTMENT ON A PARTICIPANT-BY-PARTICIPANT BASIS

The third method is to create a fee adjustment (either positive or negative) for each investment based on the amount of revenue sharing payments. Again, this not only eliminates the potential conflicts of interest and fee inequality but also lacks transparency and can be hard to communicate. Here's an example where a plan wishes to levelize administrative fees so that every participant pays 0.25 percent *through revenue sharing*. Like the prior example, Fund A pays revenue sharing of 0.50 percent, Fund B pays revenue sharing of 0.25 percent, and Fund C pays no revenue sharing. Each fund would receive a positive (i.e., increase) or negative (i.e., decrease) adjustment to its revenue sharing so that every participant pays 0.25 percent.

	Account Balance	Fund	Revenue Sharing Paid by the Participant in %	Revenue Sharing Adjustment	Net Administrative Fee (%) after Adjustments	Administrative Fees Paid by the Participant in $
Participant A	$100,000	Fund A	0.50%	−0.25%	0.25%	$250
Participant B	$100,000	Fund B	0.25%	0.00%	0.25%	$250
Participant C	$50,000	Fund C	0.00%	0.25%	0.25%	$125

Outcomes:

- Creates fee fairness and equitability.
- Lacks transparency and can be hard to communicate to participants.
- Has additional disclosure requirements.
- No ability to charge per capita fees.

OPTION #4—USE ZERO-REVENUE SHARING FUNDS

The fourth method is to use zero-revenue sharing funds and assess each participant a direct pro rata (%) or per capita ($) administrative fee. This is the simplest approach because all participants pay the same amount, and it eliminates fee inequality and potential conflicts of interest. It's similar to option 2, but it allows a plan to move to the lowest-cost share class for which the plan is eligible, which is a major argument of excessive fee cases. Here's an example where none of the funds pay revenue sharing, and all three participants are charged a per capita fee of $100:

	Account Balance	Fund	Revenue Sharing Paid by the Participant in %	Direct Per Capita Fee	Administrative Fees Paid by the Participant in $
Participant A	$100,000	Fund A	0.00%	$100	$100
Participant B	$100,000	Fund B	0.00%	$100	$100
Participant C	$50,000	Fund C	0.00%	$100	$100

Outcomes:

- Creates fee fairness and equitability.
- Makes fees transparent.
- Easy to communicate to participants.
- Provides access to lowest-cost share classes for which the plan is eligible.
- Provides flexibility in allocation methods (per capita or pro rata).

CHAPTER 15

——

Asset-Based versus Fixed Fees (Fs)

Historically, most fees have been asset based. The industry usually tries to justify this fee structure using what I call the "we take the revenue risk" argument. The provider will try to make the case that when plan assets go down, their revenue declines and when plan assets go up, their revenue increases. They will tell you the risk of revenue reduction shifts from you and your participants to them. In bad times, they will suffer, and in good times, they will benefit.

On the surface, this argument seems to have some merit and appears to make sense. But let's see how it stands up to further scrutiny. Here's a little secret the retirement industry doesn't want you to know: the primary reason a 401(k) or 403(b) plan grows is that *it's consistently funded through employee deferrals and employer contributions*! It's not because of great service or having a great investment selection and monitoring process (both of which are important). In fact, the best way to supercharge plan growth is through an optimized plan design because it increases participation and deferral rates and supercharges growth. Since contributions are made each payroll, plans rarely go down in value for extended periods, making the "we take the revenue risk" argument weak at best.

Let me illustrate with a hypothetical example. Let's use our prior example of a plan with $20 million in assets and net cash flow each year of $1 million. This means that after any rollovers or cash-outs, the combination of employee deferrals and employer contributions totals $1 million. Let's also assume an advisor is charging 0.20 percent each year for their services. And let's look at a full ten-year market cycle from 2009 to 2018 and use the annual returns of the Vanguard Target Retirement 2030 Fund Investor share (VTHRX[36]) as a proxy for the plan investment performance. To summarize, we will assume a $20 million plan is funded with $1 million per year, earns the return of the VTHRX fund each year, and pays the advisor twenty basis points for their services. Here are the results:

Year	Vanguard 2030 Fund Inv. by Year*	Total Plan Assets	Advisor Revenue	Impact on Fees	% Change
2009	26.7%	$26,317,656	$52,635	—	0.0%
2010	14.4%	$31,084,148	$62,168	Increase	18.1%
2011	-1.3%	$31,657,630	$63,315	Increase	1.8%
2012	14.2%	$37,128,405	$74,257	Increase	17.3%
2013	20.5%	$45,690,107	$91,380	Increase	23.1%
2014	7.2%	$49,915,889	$99,832	Increase	9.2%
2015	-1.0%	$50,351,073	$100,702	Increase	0.9%
2016	7.9%	$55,247,971	$110,496	Increase	9.7%
2017	17.5%	$65,861,002	$131,722	Increase	19.2%
2018	-5.9%	$62,938,026	$125,876	Decrease	-4.4%
TOTAL FEES			**$912,384**		**9.5%**

*Data provided by Morningstar. This data is for illustrative purposes only. Past performance is not indicative of future results.

So how much "revenue risk" did the advisor take? The Vanguard Fund went up in seven of ten years, which is in line with historical norms. However, you'll notice that the only year the advisor's revenue went down was 2018, when it decreased by 4.5 percent. Even in 2011 and 2015, when the fund was down (-1.3 percent and -1.0 percent, respectively), contributions caused net assets and fees to increase by 1 to 2 percent. Over the ten-year period, the advisor saw fee decreases in only one year, and their fees went up by an average of 9.5 percent per year. With the combination of positive market performance and annual funding, an asset-based fee structure is overwhelmingly in favor of service providers. The "revenue risk" argument sounds compelling but is a bit of a fallacy.

In addition, fees increased in total by 139 percent over the period, which gives rise to the possibility that fees can get out of line with the market and become unreasonable. I find this often happens when a plan is small and the fees are high from a percentage standpoint but not from an absolute dollar perspective. For example, a 12b-1 fee of 1 percent on a plan with $100,000 ($1,000 in compensation) differs greatly from a $3 million plan ($30,000 in compensation). No one pays attention, and next thing you know, the plan is a lot bigger, and the fees have spiraled out of control.

Let's compare this to a fixed-fee approach. Here, all the information is the same, except the advisor's twenty-basis-point fee has been restructured into a $40,000 fixed fee in year one (i.e., twenty basis points), and then escalates by 4 percent each year to offset the rising cost of doing business.

Year	Vanguard 2030 Fund Inv. by Year*	Total Plan Assets	Advisor Revenue	Impact on Fees	% Change
2009	26.7%	$26,304,000	$40,000.00	—	0.0%
2010	14.4%	$31,058,067	$41,600.00	Increase	4.0%
2011	−1.3%	$31,620,366	$43,264.00	Increase	4.0%
2012	14.2%	$37,078,111	$44,994.56	Increase	4.0%
2013	20.5%	$45,628,622	$46,794.34	Increase	4.0%
2014	7.2%	$49,851,528	$48,666.12	Increase	4.0%
2015	−1.0%	$50,287,445	$50,612.76	Increase	4.0%
2016	7.9%	$55,182,372	$52,637.27	Increase	4.0%
2017	17.5%	$65,795,580	$54,742.76	Increase	4.0%
2018	−5.9%	$62,883,027	$56,932.47	Increase	4.0%
Total			**$480,244.28**		**3.6%**

*Data provided by Morningstar. This data is for illustrative purposes only. Past performance is not indicative of future results.

The difference between these two scenarios is significant. With the asset-based approach, the plan paid $432,139 more in cumulative fees over the ten-year period than with the fixed-fee method. Since these fees are paid from plan assets, the cost savings would be accretive to participants, resulting in higher account balances. While the advisor saw a fee increase every year (which makes sense from an inflationary standpoint), their fees increased by only 42 percent over the period with the fixed-fee approach.

In most cases, negotiating a fixed fee is a far better approach to control the possibility of excessive fees due to the growth of plan assets. Where assets are expected to consistently decline over time (e.g., an older workforce where a lot of rollovers are expected), asset-based fees may be more appropriate. The other case is where a service provider is willing to waive its minimum fee to phase in pricing over time. For instance, from time to time, our firm has agreed to an asset-based fee with a small plan until it grows large enough to meet our minimum fee, at which point we convert to a fixed fee.

A WORD ABOUT BENCHMARKING

As I've discussed, demonstrating fee reasonableness is an important fiduciary obligation under ERISA and a major focus of litigation. But it's important to note that ERISA only requires fees be reasonable in light of the services provided, not as inexpensive as possible. In fact, the DOL tells fiduciaries not to "consider fees in a vacuum. They are only one part of the bigger picture including investment risk and returns and the extent and quality of services provided."[37] It would be simpler if ERISA defined "reasonable," but it doesn't, so another method needs to be found.

Benchmarking is the industry-standard approach to fulfilling that requirement, using "market" data for retirement plan services to ensure fair pricing. Unfortunately, Form 5500 data is typically outdated and incomplete, fee disclosure documents are too often confusing and complex, and indirect compensation like revenue sharing can misrepresent who is receiving compensation and to what extent. Plus, the process of finding meaningful comparisons is difficult and time intensive and can seem nearly impossible.

There are also very few tools and databases that can compare fees accurately and effectively. If you read the fine print of the few solutions that are available, you will often find that the information is not based on actual real-time plan data but on plan sponsor surveys, requests for proposal, standard provider fee schedules, or stale Form 5500 data. And the ones that do exist are typically sold to and through industry vendors, rather than an independent, objective resource for plan sponsors.

Even in the era of fee disclosure, the retirement industry has done a terrific job of making fees hard to decipher and understand. And most vendors want to keep it that way. Their goal is to disclose enough information to remain compliant but not nearly enough context to be held accountable and have honest conversations with their clients. That means the deck is almost always stacked against you as a plan sponsor.

Sometimes vendors will offer to benchmark your plan for free. But remember two things. First, their tools and dataset are going to be limited. And if they are willing to do it for "free," they are either using your data to make money or trying to sell you their advisory or recordkeeping/TPA services. Nobody works for free!

Several years ago, I grew frustrated with how time intensive and burdensome the process of comparing fees was for me and my clients, not to mention my concerns about data reliability, accuracy, and timeliness issues. So I created a web-based tool called

FeeMetri(k)s (FeeMetriks.com). My goal was simple—to turn any 401k or 403(b) decision maker into a fee expert in under five minutes. By giving them the data and analytics they need to know exactly what other comparable companies are paying across the industry, they can quickly and easily be sure their fees are competitive with the marketplace. And then they can leverage the data and insights to make better decisions and document their fiduciary process. I'm hopeful that one day FeeMetri(k)s will transform the industry and become the de facto solution that makes the retirement plan buying process simple, fair, and efficient.

A more time-consuming approach is to conduct a full-scope request for proposal (RFP), where you send out an extensive list of questions to multiple vendors, read through their responses, and select a few finalists who come in to present to your committee. Through that process you can gather pricing proposals using your plan demographics and service requirements so that the numbers apply specifically to the unique needs of your plan. This can be a heavy lift for everyone involved, but it's important to do from time to time. In the last chapter, I'll share ideas on how to run an effective RFP process in chapter 28.

You'll hear some folks in the industry bend the truth and claim that ERISA *requires* plans to be put out to RFP at some specific interval. But this is nonsense—there is no mention of the word "RFP" anywhere in ERISA and no prescribed frequency. However, it makes sense to regularly evaluate your fees and services to ensure you and your participants are still getting your needs met and a good return on investment. I like to use a tool like FeeMetri(k) s for annual benchmarking and then a full-scope approach every three to five years, or more often if there has been a material change to the plan assets and participants that could impact pricing (e.g., significant plan growth, M&A activity, etc.).

I'd like to make another important point about benchmarking. Part of the problem with the way the industry approaches benchmarking is that it is primarily comparison focused rather than improvement focused. I think as an industry we have misled plan sponsors into thinking the only thing that matters is whether their plan compares favorably to other plans. It's what I call the curse of the "comparison mindset." For example, plan sponsors (and their advisors) complete a benchmarking project, drop it in the fiduciary file, and check the box. But I think benchmarking should try to drive improvement and optimization, not just serve as a method to fulfill fiduciary obligations. Unfortunately, the industry provides comparison metrics they want you to see, not necessarily the ones that are most useful to you.

Favorable comparisons can make plan sponsors feel good but lull them into a false sense of security depending on the benchmark. For instance, let's say Plan A has high fees but is benchmarked against Plan B, which has *really* high fees. The fiduciaries of Plan A will probably feel good about themselves because they look good compared to Plan B. I once heard someone say that when you're getting chased by a bear, "you don't have to run faster than the bear to get away. You just have to run faster than the guy next to you." While that approach may save your life in the wilderness, I don't think it's the right mindset for a fiduciary.

Benchmarking needs to be more than just a required obligation. When there's room for meaningful improvement, it should be acted on by fiduciaries to drive the best outcomes possible. That's why you need to arm yourself with the right combination of data, detail, and context. This gives you what you need to negotiate with your vendors more effectively and increase accountability. You'll also make better decisions for your company and get the best deal possible for your people, leading to better outcomes over time. When you're in control, you can make sure you never get "sold" a high-cost 401k or 403(b) plan by the retirement industry again.

CASE STUDY

In 2016, we were hired by a company whose plan had $97 million in assets and approximately one thousand participants. They had never used an advisor before and used a top-tier recordkeeper. All fees were asset based. The all-in fees for the plan were approximately 0.62 percent, or about $600,000 per year. This included average fund fees of approximately 0.42 percent, or $400,000, and recordkeeping fees of roughly 0.15 percent, or $147,000, generated through the use of revenue sharing.

We gathered blind bids from three other well-known recordkeepers to establish a clear baseline for where the market priced the plan at the time using current demographics. We requested fixed-fee bids, which ranged from 0.08 percent and 0.12 percent, or $98 to $110 per participant. The incumbent recordkeeper had done a good job and was allowed to rebid, responding with an initial offer of 0.12 percent, or $118 per participant.

Using the other bids, we negotiated on behalf of the committee, reaching a final offer from the incumbent of 0.10 percent, or $100 per participant, saving the plan roughly $50,000 in annual recordkeeping fees. In addition, we redesigned the fund lineup, eliminating revenue sharing and reducing the average fund expense to 0.17 percent, or approximately $160,000.

At the time these changes were implemented, all-in fees had been reduced to 0.32 percent, or approximately $312,000 per year, an annual savings of nearly $300,000. We also created a five-year projection that assumed the plan would grow to $155 million. By reducing the fees and moving to a fixed-fee approach, we estimated that all-in plan fees would drop to 0.27 percent over five years, achieving cumulative savings of more than $2 million. Using a discount rate of 4 percent, we projected the present value of those savings would be roughly $1.7 million, or about $1,650 per employee.

By the end of 2019, the plan had performed better than our original projections, growing to approximately $151 million and 1,300 employees. Meanwhile, all-in fees had dropped to 0.24 percent, or roughly $360,000 per year. While the plan assets had grown by more than 50 percent, and plan participants had increased by almost 30 percent, average fund fees had fallen all the way to 0.12 percent, while recordkeeping fees had been reduced to 0.09 percent. Total fees from our original implementation had only increased by 15 percent ($312,000 to $360,000).

Let me put this into perspective and ask you a question. If I was able to save your company $1.7 million over the next five years in IT or health insurance costs, would you be interested? Of course you would! That's because these types of expenses directly impact your bottom line and profitability, unlike most retirement plan expenses that are indirect and paid from the plan itself, not by the company. And because of this, I've found that companies tend to be less vigilant about controlling costs. That's a mistake. As a fiduciary, you should be just as discerning about your retirement spending as you are with the rest of your business.

3
Fs
Fee Structure

SUMMARY

- The three largest excessive fee lawsuits (Lockheed Martin, Boeing, and ABB) were settled for a total of $174 million, and attorney's fees equated to approximately 30 percent, or $55 million.
- In 2018, the Center for Retirement Research at Boston College found that there were over 100 new 401(k) lawsuits filed and that of the roughly 430 cases they evaluated, 60 percent were still pending, 20 percent were dismissed/closed, 16 percent were settled/decided, and 4 percent were on appeal.
- AllianceBernstein found in 2014 that 37 percent of 1,000 plan sponsors surveyed were unaware of their fiduciary status, and 6 percent were unsure.
- The DOL has estimated that high retirement fees can reduce a person's account balance by 28 percent.

- Determine what services your plan and your participants need.
- Decide the fee to pay for each service and benchmark these amounts to ensure they are reasonable in light of the services being provided.
- Determine how fees will be paid, either allocated directly to participant accounts or indirectly through revenue sharing or paid directly by the company.
- If allocated directly to participant accounts, determine whether the fees will be allocated as a flat fee (per capita) or in proportion to their account balance (pro rata). If allocated indirectly to participant accounts through revenue sharing, determine which share classes are appropriate and make sure to use one of the fee levelization methods described.
- Develop a strategy for communicating fees and payment methods to employees.
- Document the process.
- Benchmark fees annually to ensure reasonableness using a tool like FeeMetri(k)s.
- Conduct an RFP process every three to five years or when material changes have impacted your plan.

1. Are you satisfied with the level of fee transparency your service providers have provided to your committee?
2. Are your recordkeeper, TPA, and advisory fees asset based or fixed?
3. Do you apply these fees on a pro rata or per capita basis?
4. Have you conducted an allocation study to determine the most prudent method of allocating fees?
5. Does your plan use revenue sharing to offset administrative costs?
6. Have you levelized revenue sharing to avoid fee inequality and conflicts of interest? If so, which of the four methods do you use?
7. Do you regularly benchmark your plan's fees to ensure reasonableness?
8. Have you created a present-value calculation to estimate the amount of fees your plan is projected to pay over the next five to ten years?
9. Have you documented your fee decision-making process?

4

Ip

Investment Process

CHAPTER 16

IPS Best Practices (Ip)

Antoine de Saint-Exupéry was a French writer, poet, aristocrat, journalist, and pioneering aviator. He became a laureate of several of France's highest literary awards and also won the United States National Book Award. Prior to World War II, he achieved fame in France as an aviator and joined the French Air Force at the start of the war, flying reconnaissance missions until France's armistice with Germany in 1940.

He once said that "a goal without a plan is just a wish," which is fitting since he was a pilot. To successfully fly a plane, you need a flight plan and flight path that constantly adjusts to remain on the course. Without it, you don't have a way to determine whether you're headed in the right direction.

When managing plan investments, an investment policy statement (IPS) serves as your flight plan. I believe a written investment policy is the only way to demonstrate a thoughtful process and make well-informed, prudent investment decisions consistent with the fiduciary requirements imposed by ERISA.

For a committee, this starts with developing the overall investment policy approach, including the investment selection and monitoring process. It culminates with a written IPS.

As part of the process, the committee needs to determine the most appropriate asset classes in the plan's core investment lineup based on the demographics of its employee population, and it needs to streamline the complexity often faced by plan participants. Once these decisions have been made, the committee needs to consistently follow the processes outlined in the IPS regarding the selection, monitoring, and replacement/removal of the individual fund options.

Although ERISA doesn't require an IPS, the law makes it clear in Section 402(b)(1) that plans must "provide a procedure for establishing and carrying out a funding policy in a method consistent with the objectives of the plan."

Furthermore, the DOL has stated in Interpretive Bulletin (IB) 2016-1 that "a statement of investment policy designed to further the purposes of the plan and its funding policy is consistent with the fiduciary obligations in ERISA Section 404(a)(1)(A) and (B)" that fiduciaries are required to fulfill the duty of prudence to participants and beneficiaries. It's also one of the first items requested when the DOL audits a retirement plan.

While the law doesn't technically require an IPS, the DOL (which has enforcement authority for ERISA) says having one is consistent with the fiduciary obligations set forth under the law. Nothing like a catch-22 for managing legal risk.

An IPS is a useful tool to help fiduciaries demonstrate they've followed a prudent process when selecting and monitoring plan investments. A well-constructed IPS establishes guidelines for selecting and monitoring plan investments, while providing a framework for making critical fiduciary decisions.

While IPS usage is increasing, not every plan uses one, especially in the small plan space, where best practices get adopted much less frequently. According to the 2018 PLANSPONSOR Defined Contribution Survey (which included roughly 4,000 responses), the following percentage of plan sponsors (based on plan size) had a written IPS for their defined contribution plans:

All Industries

Overall	<$5m	$5m-$50m	$50m-$200m	>$200m
68.9%	46.2%	72.4%	85.3%	89.9%

However, based on my experience, not every IPS is created equal. Many plans have an IPS that's likely creating more fiduciary risk, not less. Many plans take what I call the check-the-box approach to IPS management. This often happens when someone at the company involved with the plan (e.g., a CFO or VP of HR) reads an article that says they need an IPS for their 401(k) plan. So they Google "IPS," find a boilerplate template, and download it. Or they ask one of their service providers, who happily obliges and sends along a generic version. In both cases, what typically happens is the IPS gets stuck in a file (often without reading it or verifying that it can be followed), and the person checks the box. In fact, I'd venture a guess that many of the companies who answered affirmatively to the PLANSPONSOR survey have a check-the-box IPS.

Any ERISA attorney in the country will tell you it's better to have no process at all than one you don't follow. A case in point is the

2012 ruling from *Tussey v. ABB Inc.* In that case, ABB had implemented an IPS but failed to follow the terms of the document, which led, in part, to its initial loss in court and a $55 million judgment in favor of the plaintiffs (i.e., the plan participants).

As an alternative to the common check-the-box approach, here are seven tips for creating a well-constructed IPS:

1. Make sure your IPS describes the purpose, roles, and responsibilities of those involved with the plan (e.g., committee members, recordkeepers/TPAs, investment advisors, etc.); factors that will be used to select and monitor investments and expenses; and the process for reviewing/replacing underperforming investments (often referred to as a watch list). Also, make sure the IPS is signed.
2. Beware of drafting the IPS with language that's too broad (potentially rendering the document useless) or too strict (making it difficult to comply with, like in the *Tussey* case). You want enough detail and structure to provide a clear process to follow but enough flexibility to maneuver. Fred Reish has noted that a properly constructed IPS should be a "framework for making decisions, not a mandate."
3. Words like "always" or "never" or "required" should be avoided. Also, replace words like "annually" with "periodically." For instance, instead of saying, "The IPS will be reviewed annually" (which creates a strict frequency of review), say, "The IPS will be reviewed periodically." It's still a good idea to review it annually or biannually.
4. Select and monitor investments using quantitative criteria, but make decisions using a qualitative process. At Greenspring Advisors, we use quantitative criteria to score and rank plan investments. When an investment fails a certain number of criteria, it goes on the watch list, and our team conducts

further due diligence to identify what caused the failure. If necessary, we then make the change if we are an ERISA 3(38) fiduciary or make our recommendation if we are a 3(21) fiduciary. We describe the quantitative criteria as the Check Engine light in your car—it tells you something is wrong with your vehicle but not the problem. The qualitative process is like taking the car to a mechanic, who then plugs it into the computer and pulls the error codes to determine whether the issue is a minor or major one.

5. Make sure you have the right tools and technology in place to monitor the criteria stated in the IPS. I commonly read through existing investment policy statements that obligate plan sponsors to monitor or measure investments using specific criteria but with no tools to do so or any evidence the process has been followed (e.g., reports, minutes, etc.). Remember, not having a process at all is better than having a process that isn't followed.

6. When an underperforming fund qualifies for the watch list, make sure to document the factors that influence any decisions to keep, remove, or replace it. This should be reflected in the meeting minutes or other written format.

7. Periodically (usually every couple of years), have the committee read through the IPS and discuss the various sections to ensure everyone understands what it says and to determine if any modifications are warranted due to a change in process or procedure. In reality, your IPS should not change often.

Remember that a well-constructed IPS is simply a tool in the fiduciary's toolbox. Like any tool, if it's in the hands of an expert, it can be used for great benefit. In the hands of a novice, however, it's likely to do significant damage.

CHAPTER 17

Emerging Trends in Fund Menu Design (Ip)

To say that 401(k) and 403(b) investing has shifted over the past decade would be an understatement. The power of the default effect in automatic enrollment plans has made target date funds (TDFs) the dominant investment choice for retirement savers.

I highlighted the exponential growth of TDFs in chapter 8. The simplicity and professional management of TDFs makes them hard to beat. For instance, JPMorgan's 2016 participant survey highlighted the following percentage of participants who found TDFs and reenrollment appealing:[38]

	Under 30 Years Old	30 Years and Over
Appeal of TDFs*	97%	87%
Reenrollment	93%	79%

*Appeal of TDF % shows those who find TDFs "somewhat" or "very" appealing.

While both groups embraced TDFs, what's most interesting is that younger participants proved to be the most powerful advocates for these types of solutions.

We found a similar statistic in our 2019 employee survey.[39] Overall, 75 percent of respondents preferred to use a TDF instead of a DIY approach, with women (80 percent), younger workers (79 percent), and those earning less than $50,000 (80 percent) the most supportive.

Given the shift in participant mindset and demographics, it's important for retirement plan committees to rethink the traditional approach to designing investment menus. In fact, I believe the target date decision is the most important investment choice for this generation of retirement plan fiduciaries. But first, let's take a step back and discuss the strategic outcomes fiduciaries should focus on when designing a fund lineup for their plan.

FIDUCIARY CONSIDERATIONS

In Section of 404(a) of ERISA, the first two fiduciary duties are referred to as the "duty of exclusive purpose" and the "duty of prudence." The regulation states that fiduciaries must perform their duties solely in the interest of the participants and beneficiaries, and for the exclusive purpose of providing benefits to them and with the care, skill, prudence, and diligence of someone who is an expert. This is why it's so important for retirement plan committee members to stay up to date on the latest research, trends, and best practices evolving within the industry. Flexibility is key. How can fiduciaries fulfill their obligations if their approach and mindset are static while techniques are dynamic and improving?

For instance, in the mid- to late 1960s, when open-heart surgery was first introduced at the Cleveland Clinic, 9 percent of the first 150 patients who received the procedure died before they were released from the hospital![40] Today, even though the patient population is becoming older and operative risk is higher, the mortality rate is only between 1 and 3 percent. This is because of surgeons (and other members of the medical community) who have refined the procedure, developed new products and innovative techniques, improved postoperative rehab, and enhanced the overall diagnosis, treatment, and standard of care. Imagine a heart surgeon performing a procedure as if it was still the 1960s. Is that who you'd want operating on you? Probably not. So why choose antiquated fiduciary practices?

BEHAVIORAL FINANCE CONCEPTS

Richard Thaler, an American economist and theorist in behavioral economics at the University of Chicago Booth School of Business, won the 2017 Nobel Prize in Economics for his contributions to the science of behavioral economics. He and Cass Sunstein coined the term *choice architecture* in their 2008 book *Nudge: Improving Decisions about Health, Wealth, and Happiness*. It refers to the practice of influencing choice by changing the manner in which options are presented to people.

The historical approach to fund menu design was to provide participants with lots of choices and assume they would make good decisions. However, the economic theory behind this approach (i.e., people will make optional choices for themselves) has been shown to be flawed in the real world by the concept of choice overload, also referred to as overchoice. This phenomenon occurs when people have too many choices. It leads to increased complexity and has been associated with unhappiness, decision fatigue, and choice deferral (e.g., not making a choice altogether or delaying the process of choosing). When faced with choice overload, most people make worse decisions, not better ones.

The impact of overchoice has been studied in 401(k) plans. In their 2010 paper titled "Choice Proliferation, Simplicity Seeking, and Asset Allocation," researchers Sheena S. Iyengar and Emir Kamenica found that for every ten investment options in a plan, participation decreases by 2 percent, and equity allocation decreases by 3.28 percent. There's also a concurrent increase of 2.87 percent that the participant will allocate nothing to equities.[41] Behaviorally speaking, an investment lineup with ten choices is likely to be far more effective regarding enhanced asset allocation and participation than one with twenty or thirty options. Their primary conclusion was that "a larger choice set increases the appeal of simple, easy-to-understand, options."

Despite a large number of options in workplace retirement plans, the average number of funds used is small, and the vast majority of DIY investors do not rebalance their portfolio consistently, signaling a lack of engagement. Following a disciplined rebalancing approach has proven essential to successful investment experiences and is a hallmark of TDFs, which automatically rebalance for the participant. According to research by Vanguard:

1. The average number of funds offered (target date and target risk counting as one option) is eighteen, and the median number of funds offered is sixteen.
2. The average number of funds used by participants is only 2.5, and the median number of funds used is one.
3. In 2017, only 12 percent of DIY participants (i.e., non-TDF users) traded in their account or rebalanced their investments.
4. Overall, 10 percent of participants had extreme asset allocations (100 percent equity or 0 percent equity). These extreme

allocations have fallen significantly over recent years due to the rise in the popularity of TDFs. In 2010, 22 percent of Vanguard participants had extreme allocations.[42]

Faced with the high standard of care required by ERISA and informed by the growing body of behavioral research that shows participants make poor decisions, how should retirement plan committees respond?

First, it's important to recognize that fiduciaries exercise an enormous influence on both the choices their participants will make and the outcomes they will experience. If you are a Spider-Man fan, you'll appreciate Peter Parker's frequent memory of what his uncle Ben told him, that "with great power, comes great responsibility!"

I believe that forward-thinking retirement plan committees should embrace the idea that they are choice architects whose primary responsibility is to design fund menus that are user friendly for participants and improve their probability of making good choices. The foundation of successful investment experiences is influenced by three factors: asset allocation, diversification, and costs.

ASSET ALLOCATION

Vanguard has suggested that 85.5 percent of a portfolio's variability in returns comes from asset allocation or the ratio/mix of asset classes, such as stocks, bonds, and cash within a portfolio. The remaining 14.5 percent comes from security selection and market timing.[43] This aligns with other studies that have been conducted over the years.[44]

Given the longtime horizon of investors, following a long-term investment orientation consistent with retirement plan investing is essential.

DIVERSIFICATION

Constructing a portfolio that maintains consistent exposure to multiple asset classes is an important strategy that reduces the risks associated with a particular company, sector, or country. Harry Markowitz, an American economist and winner of the 1990 Nobel Prize in Economics, called diversification "the only free lunch in investing."

Markets and asset classes perform and behave differently at various times. For instance, both US and non-US equities offer the potential to earn positive expected returns over long time periods, but they may perform differently over shorter durations. Further, there is no reliable evidence that anyone can consistently predict this performance ahead of time. Given this, I believe that a retirement plan investment strategy should use the global opportunity set available to deliver diversification benefits and potentially higher-than-expected returns.

COSTS

In most areas of life, there's a correlation between price and quality. For example, if I buy a $65,000 Mercedes E-Class, I should expect better quality than a $25,000 entry-level Honda Accord.

However, with mutual fund performance, the data shows an inverse relationship between costs and outcomes. I'll highlight this in more detail in chapter 19.

CHAPTER 18

———

Target Date Fund Selection and Monitoring (Ip)

With the passage of the Pension Protection Act of 2006 (PPA), target date funds (TDFs) exploded in popularity and have become the de facto qualified default investment alternative (QDIA), with nearly three-quarters of plan sponsors using this option.[45] As I mentioned in chapter 8, TDF assets have grown to approximately $1.7 trillion at the end of 2019 according to Morningstar. Further, Cerulli Associates expects TDFs to capture 85 percent of new cash flows into 401(k) plans by 2021.

While the QDIA regulation provides a "safe harbor" that protects fiduciaries from liability for their decisions, it only applies if they comply with all the requirements of the regulation, which includes prudently selecting and monitoring the investment used as the QDIA.

Given the explosive growth of TDFs, the DOL issued a bulletin in February 2013 titled "Target Date Funds—Tips for ERISA Plan Fiduciaries" to provide guidance to plan fiduciaries and clarify what types of things they should consider when selecting a TDF solution.[46] This bulletin outlined the following eight steps that plan fiduciaries should take when evaluating TDFs:

1. Establish a process for comparing and selecting TDFs.
2. Establish a process for the periodic review of selected TDFs.
3. Understand the fund's investments—the allocation in different asset classes (e.g., stocks, bonds, and cash), individual investments, and how these will change over time.
4. Review the fund's fees and investment expenses.
5. Inquire about whether a custom or nonproprietary TDF would be a better fit for your plan.
6. Develop effective employee communications.
7. Take advantage of available sources of information to evaluate the TDF and recommendations you received regarding the TDF selection.
8. Document the process.

When the DOL speaks, it is important to take note. I'd suggest reading the publication for additional details.

In my experience, most plan sponsors have not selected TDFs based on an "objective, thorough, and analytical process" as specified by the DOL for two primary reasons. First, the selection has often been tied to the choice of plan provider, with little thought given to whether the TDF was right for the plan. Second, few consultants or advisors have developed a methodology or the technical expertise to guide the process for plan fiduciaries. With enhanced scrutiny by regulators, the evolving needs of participants, and the proliferation and complexity of TDF options in the marketplace, the DOL has also stated, "Within this general framework, however, there are considerable differences among TDFs offered by different providers, even among TDFs with the same target date. For example, TDFs may have different investment strategies, glide paths, and investment-related fees. Because these differences can significantly affect the way a TDF performs, it is important that fiduciaries understand these differences when selecting a TDF as an investment option for their plan."

Here are four signs it may be time to review your plan's TDF:

1. Your TDF and your plan provider are the same (e.g., Vanguard, Fidelity, T. Rowe Price).

2. You have never gone through an "objective, thorough, and analytical" process regarding your TDF.

3. You don't have any written documentation that includes how you reached decisions about the choice of TDF.

4. You cannot easily explain the "glide path" of your plan's TDF.

CHAPTER 19

======

The Evidence for Passive
Management (Ip)

Greenspring Advisors has embraced an evidence-based approach to investing since we opened our doors in 2004. Despite beginning my career working for a major brokerage firm where I was indoctrinated with the idea that active management was the only way to invest, I started using exchange-traded funds (ETFs) for my clients on a very limited basis even back then. This was in the early days, before the dramatic rise in popularity of these types of investment vehicles. Still, there was something about low-cost index investing that made sense to me.

After leaving to start Greenspring, I was introduced to a robust body of research that had never been shown to me at my prior firm. The evidence I encountered compelled me to go all in on passive management for both our corporate retirement plan and wealth management clients. It was like Neo taking the red pill in *The Matrix*.

Passive management (often referred to as indexing) is not a great descriptor. So let me explain the difference between this style of investing and the traditional approach, which is often referred to as active management. The primary goal for active managers is to beat the market by taking advantage of pricing "mistakes." It's an attempt to predict the future. This approach to investing is predicated on the idea that markets are broken and can be exploited by portfolio managers and research analysts who can consistently outsmart the millions of other investors they're competing with daily, otherwise known as the market. But investing is a zero-sum game. Too often, this approach proves costly and fruitless. Predictions don't come to fruition, and managers miss the strong returns that markets provide because they hold the wrong securities at the wrong time.

Passive managers accept that markets are efficient, which means they incorporate and reflect all available information. They also accept that trying to forecast or outguess the millions of other investors is both costly and futile. Instead, most passive managers try to track the returns of a particular market index or benchmark as closely as possible instead of outperforming it.

The difference between the return of the index and the return of the fund should be close to the fund expenses. To be clear, indexing and passive management, while often used synonymously, are not always the same. For instance, all index funds could be considered passively managed, but not all passively managed funds are considered index funds. But that's a topic for another day.

EXAMINING THE EVIDENCE

Let's shift gears and examine the evidence for passive investing. Significant amounts of empirical data show that most active investment managers don't outperform their respective benchmark indexes on a year-to-year basis because of factors such as poor security selection, failed market-timing strategies, and high costs.

Standard & Poor's publishes its S&P Indices Versus Active (SPIVA) scorecard, a robust, widely referenced research piece that compares managed funds against their appropriate benchmarks semiannually. S&P provides scorecard reporting on managed funds in the US, Australia, Canada, Europe, India, Japan, Latin America, and South Africa. The SPIVA scorecard has more than fifteen years of published data surveying more than ten thousand managed funds around the world. Its persistence report shows how consistent returns are over time for active fund managers and whether they can consistently deliver above-average returns over multiple periods.

Unfortunately for active managers, S&P has found that most have historically underperformed their benchmarks over both short- and long-term periods. This phenomenon has tended to hold true (with a few exceptions) across countries and regions. Another important observation is that even when most actively managed funds have outperformed the benchmark over one time period, the outperformance usually fails to persist over multiple periods.

Another challenge investor's face is that funds disappear at a meaningful rate, usually because of poor results or low asset accumulation. Survivorship bias is the "tendency to view the performance of existing stocks or funds in the market as a representative comprehensive sample without regarding those that have gone bust."[47] This phenomenon, which is widespread in the investment industry, results in an overestimation of the past returns of mutual funds. The nice thing about the SPIVA is that it factors in all the funds that existed during its research, not just the survivors, which eliminates survivorship bias.

Using data from the SPIVA scorecard, this chart shows the percentage of actively managed equity funds by asset class that failed to beat the index over the previous five-, ten-, and fifteen-year time periods, ending December 31, 2018.

SPIVA Data

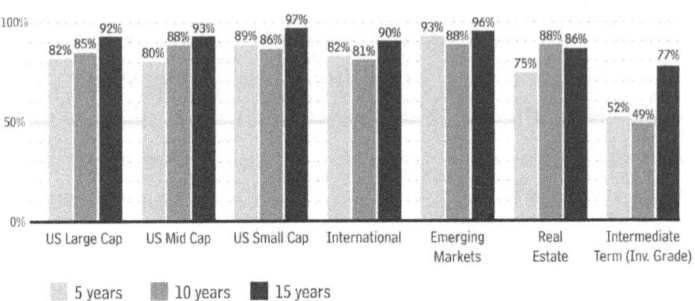

Source: *SPIVA US Year-End 2018 Scorecard*, S&P Dow Jones Indices, 2019, https://www.spglobal.com/_assets/documents/corporate/us-spiva-report-11-march-2019.pdf.

Apart from intermediate-term bond funds over the three- and five-year periods, the vast majority of active funds across all asset classes failed to outperform. For instance, over the past fifteen years, 92 percent of US large cap funds, 93 percent of US mid-cap funds, and 97 percent of small cap funds have failed to beat the benchmark for their respective asset class. It doesn't get much better using active funds that invest outside the US, as 90 percent of international funds and 96 percent of emerging market funds have also failed to beat the index over that same period.

These charts show both the survivorship and the success rate of both equity and fixed-income mutual funds over ten, fifteen, and twenty years, ending December 31, 2018. There were 3,097 equity funds and 1,515 bond funds in the sample as of the beginning of the period. During that time, the success rate (i.e., funds that existed the entire twenty-year period and beat their respective benchmarks) was only 23 percent for equity funds and 8 percent for bond funds.

Further, at the end of the period, only about 40 percent of the funds in each asset class remained in existence for the full twenty-year period.

DFA Equity Survivorship

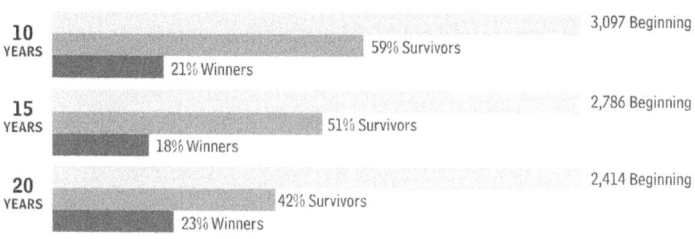

US-based equity fund performance periods ending December 31, 2018

DFA Fixed Income Survivorship

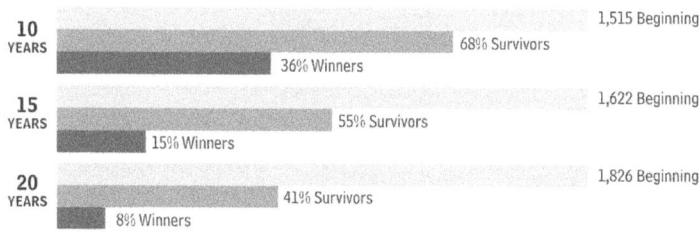

US-based fixed income fund performance periods ending December 31, 2018

Source: Dimensional Fund Advisors (DFA). Each sample includes funds at the beginning of the five-, ten-, and fifteen-year periods, ending December 31, 2018. Survivors are funds that had returns for every month in the sample period. Winners are funds that survived and outperformed their respective Morningstar category benchmark over the period. US-domiciled open-end mutual fund data is from Morningstar and the Center for Research in Security Prices (CRSP) from the University of Chicago.

With more than ten thousand funds available for purchase within the marketplace, trying to find those precious few that will outperform is a tough job. Many investors, committee members, and advisors/consultants focus on funds that have strong track records, assuming past performance is evidence these managers will continue to outpace their benchmarks (despite all the compliance disclaimers to the contrary).

But is this assumption backed by reliable evidence? The data suggest otherwise. This chart illustrates the lack of persistence in outperformance through December 31, 2018. At the end of each year, equity funds were sorted within their category based on their five-year total return. The tables show the percentage of funds in the top quartile (25 percent) of five-year performance that subsequently ranked in the top quartile of one-year performance in the following year.

For example, from 2014 to 2018, only 25 percent of equity funds were also ranked in the top quartile of performance in their category in both the previous periods (2004–2008 and 2009–2013).

DFA Persistence

EQUITY FUNDS

TOP 25%	2004-2008	28%
	2005-2009	23%
	2006-2010	23%
	2007-2011	18%
	2008-2012	16%
	2009-2013	14%
	2010-2014	18%
	2011-2015	22%
	2012-2016	21%
	2013-2017	23%
	2014-2018	26%

Previous 5 years   Following 5 years   100%

21%
AVERAGE

Source: Dimensional Fund Advisors (DFA). At the end of each year, funds are sorted within their category based on their five-year total return. The exhibit shows the percentage of funds in the top quartile (25 percent) of five-year performance that ranked in the top quartile of performance over the following five years. For example, in 2014–2018, for equity funds ranked in the top quartile of performance in their category in the previous period (2009–2013), only 25 percent also ranked in the top quartile in the subsequent period (2014–2018). (US-domiciled, open-end mutual fund data is from Morningstar. Past performance is no guarantee of future results.)

Given the data, I believe the emphasis that retirement plan committees place on hiring an advisor/consultant that they think can identify managers who will beat or outperform the market is misplaced at best and is disastrous at worst. There will, in fact, be a small number of managers who outperform over time. I just don't believe that any advisory firm, regardless of the resources at their disposal, can consistently identify those managers ahead of time who will outperform in the future with any reliability. That includes my firm.

Most advisors/consultants are loath to admit this. However, to support this idea even more, take a look at Amit Goyal and Sumit Wahal's 2005 study, *The Selection and Termination of Investment Management Firms by Plan Sponsors*. The study evaluated 8,755 hiring decisions over a ten-year period (1994–2003). On average, the pension funds surveyed chose managers who generated significant excess returns over their benchmark index in the three years immediately before hiring (2.91 percent), only to find that they couldn't replicate this outperformance in the corresponding future three-year period (–0.47 percent). Again, the data show that past performance has little relevance on future returns, and neither committees nor their consultants have avoided this trap.

Selection and Termination of Managers

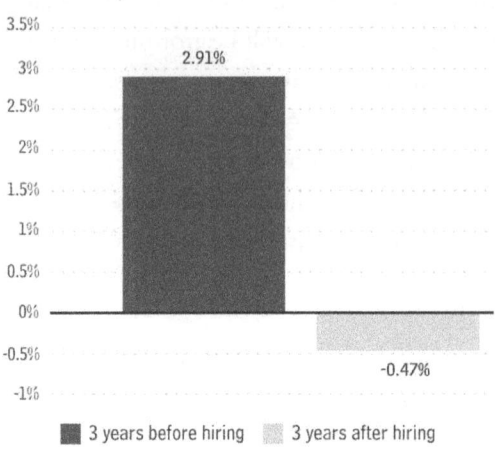

One area I think can have an important impact on future out-performance is costs, at least from a peer-group standpoint. For instance, in 2002, mutual fund industry insiders hired Financial Research Corporation (FRC) to complete a study to find a predictor of future fund performance. The study, *Predicting Mutual Fund Performance II: After The Bear*, measured ten predictors (e.g., past performance, Morningstar ratings, expenses, net sales, asset size, risk/volatility measures), and the findings showed that most of the statistics had no predictive value. The study did, however, find one reliable predictor—expenses. Funds with lower expenses delivered "above-average future performance across nearly all time periods." FRC concluded that a favorable expense ratio is an "exceptional predictor" for bonds and a "good predictor" for stock funds.

In addition, a 2010 Morningstar article research report titled "How Expense Ratios and Star Ratings Predict Success" concluded:

> If there's anything in the whole world of mutual funds that you can take to the bank, it's that expense ratios help you make a better

decision. In every single time period and data point tested, low-cost funds beat high-cost funds. Expense ratios are strong predictors of performance. In every asset class over every time period, the cheapest quintile produced higher total returns than the most expensive quintile. *Investors should make expense ratios a primary test in fund selection. They are still the most dependable predictor of performance. Start by focusing on funds in the cheapest or two cheapest quintiles, and you'll be on the path to success.* [Emphasis mine]

Ironically, investment performance plays a small role in driving successful retirement outcomes for participants, even though retirement plan committees and advisors/consultants focus heavily on this area. Instead, factors like plan design and plan funding have been shown to be much more important drivers of retirement sufficiency.

I believe retirement plan committees would be well served by embracing a low-cost, passive investment approach and by shifting their time and effort to areas that move the needle for their participants in a more significant way. This doesn't mean that having a robust investment selection and monitoring process is unimportant. On the contrary, ERISA mandates the need for this.

CHAPTER 20

Putting Investment Theory into Practice (Ip)

So far, I've discussed a lot of theory, research, and data. Now I'd like to put forth a practical framework plan fiduciaries can use. I outline a tiered approach to fund lineup design, with each tier assigned a priority level (highest to lowest), the investment option to use ("What"), important considerations and recommendations ("How"), and a target outcome.

For retirement plan committees seeking simplicity, tiers 1 and 2 offer the best approach. But don't mistake simple with unsophisticated. Tiers 3 and 4 provide enhanced diversification opportunities and additional choice but with higher complexity. Tier 5 introduces additional customization opportunities for participants but at a higher cost. Tier 6 adds maximum flexibility but increases complexity and may lead to suboptimal outcomes and poor decision-making.

#				
1	Highest	QDIA/default option	Low-cost TDF, balanced fund, or managed account solution.	Simplified user experience.
			If TDF, consider whether to use off-the-shelf or custom option, per DOL.	Minimal flexibility.
			The preferred approach for most participants in the plan.	High probability of improved decision-making.
			Consider implementing reenrollment to get participants prudently positioned as a starting point.	
2	High	"Core" asset class funds	Should include six to ten equity and fixed-income funds, spanning both domestic and international markets.	
			Serves as portfolio building blocks for DIY investors (i.e., non-TDF users).	
			Broad-based index funds are good choices.	
			Seek to minimize overlap— one fund per asset class.	
3	Moderate	Style-based and/ or alternative asset class funds	Value versus growth options.	Enhanced diversification opportunities
			Can include emerging markets, real estate, etc.	
4	Low to moderate	Risk-based model portfolios	Five to six prepackaged portfolios based on risk (e.g., aggressive, balanced, conservative, etc.) using underlying funds from the core menu	Additional choice
5	Low	Managed account service	Typically provided by a recordkeeper (proprietary) or third party, like Financial Engines, Morningstar, etc.	Personalization. Higher cost.
			Beware of high fees.	
			Can often function as a glorified TDF in terms of performance.	
			Typically, low adoption among participants unless used as the QDIA/default option.	

6	Lowest	Brokerage window	Provides substantial choice to participants.	Maximum flexibility.
			Used by very few people.	High risk of suboptimal outcomes.
			Not recommended because of negative outcomes and fiduciary considerations.	

Retirement plan committees play an important role in shaping the financial futures of their employees. Small decisions can have an enormous impact on outcomes, especially over long periods of time, like a person's entire career. It's important for fiduciaries to use the latest available information, research, and techniques to design an investment lineup that ensures a high probability of success for plan participants and beneficiaries. With hope, this framework serves as a starting point for you.

CASE STUDY

In 2016, we were hired by an architecture firm to take over for a prior advisor.

The plan had fifty-five investment options with only six index funds. There was also significant asset class overlap and redundancy (there were ten large cap funds alone). There was no IPS. Furthermore, of the fifty-five options, twenty-three failed our investment due diligence screens and qualified for the watch list. Additionally, less than 30 percent of assets were in professionally managed options. It's safe to say that we had our work cut out for us.

Our first step was to put a formal IPS in place. Next, we analyzed the plan's TDF solution and selected a new option. We also reduced their fund lineup to thirteen index-based options (using one fund per asset class), cutting fund expenses from 0.47

percent to 0.14 percent today. We also implemented a TDF reen-rollment. Four years later, 99 percent of the assets are still in these options. Using the IPS as a guide, we've provided due diligence reporting versus our stated criteria at every committee meeting since that time.

It turned out that even architects needed help building some things. Luckily, we were there when they needed us.

4

Ip

Investment Process

SUMMARY

- In 2017, Vanguard found that only 12 percent of DIY participants (i.e., non-TDF users) traded in their account or rebalanced their investments.
- In 2016, JPMorgan found that TDFs appealed to 97 percent of participants under age thirty and 87 percent of participants over age thirty.
- Cerulli Associates projects that TDFs will capture 85 percent of all 401(k) cash flows by 2021.
- In 2010, researchers found that for every ten investment options in a plan, participation decreases by 2 percent, equity allocation decreases by 3.28 percent, and there's a concurrent increase of 2.87 percent that the participant will allocate nothing to equities.
- According to the SPIVA scorecard, more than 90 percent of active managers across global asset classes have failed to outperform their respective benchmark index over the past fifteen years, ending December 31, 2018.
- Over the past fifteen years, ending December 31, 2018, Dimen-

sional Fund Advisors (DFA) found that, on average, only 21percent of equity funds were also ranked in the top quartile of performance in their category in rolling five-year periods.

- A 2010 Morningstar study found that in every single time period and data point tested, low-cost funds beat high-cost funds.

- Create an IPS specifically tailored to the needs of your plan and the monitoring capabilities of your committee.
- Use mostly (if not all) passive/index investments.
- Make sure every plan investment has an expense ratio in the top quartile (or better) of its peer group.
- Streamline your fund lineup to no more than ten to fifteen options (TDFs count as one).
- Select a TDF using an objective, thorough, and analytical process.

1. Do you have an IPS?
2. Has it been specifically customized for your plan, or is it a check-the-box version?
3. Are most of the investment options in your plan active or passive/index?
4. Do you have too many investment options in your plan, contributing to overchoice for your participants?
5. Are your TDF provider and recordkeeper the same?
6. Were your TDFs selected according to the DOL's recommended guidance?

5

Ps

Participant Support

CHAPTER 21

Financial Wellness versus Financial Well-Being (Ps)

Did you know that chronic stress literally kills your brain, impacting its ability to concentrate, think clearly, and act decisively, and leading to memory loss and heightened emotional reactions? French researchers discovered an enzyme that, when triggered by stress, attacks a molecule in the hippocampus, the part of the brain involved in the formation of new memories and associated with learning and emotions.[48] This leads to fewer neural connections, cognitive impairment, and can even alter social behavior. Not surprisingly, financial stress is on the rise.

The concept of employee engagement has been reframed into a discussion about "financial wellness" over the last several years. It's become a hot topic in the retirement industry, and employers recognize that employee financial well-being can have a positive impact on employee satisfaction, productivity, and overall engagement.

The term *financial wellness* is hard to define and is an overused buzzword within the industry.[49] In many cases, the current state of financial wellness solutions and initiatives have been heavily content focused in areas such as retirement saving, budgeting, and debt management.

However, financial wellness needs to be more comprehensive than educational content or a set of self-service online tools because employees still want (and need) human interaction and actual advice from a qualified advisor. True financial wellness should create a stronger financial foundation for employees that leads to clear, actionable strategies combined with better financial behaviors, resulting in improved financial health.

In May 2019, our firm conducted a comprehensive survey across our client base that was aimed at providing a multidimensional assessment of employee perceptions of their financial well-being.[50] The survey included more than seventy questions in ten different categories, and we received responses from 1,872 US-based employees throughout our corporate retirement plan client base. The average completion time for the survey was eleven minutes and forty-five seconds, and the average completion rate was 89 percent. It required respondents to provide the name of their company, but other than that, the survey was anonymous.

Throughout the survey, we used gender, age, and income as the dimensions to categorize and analyze the data. I list the survey demographics here.

Gender

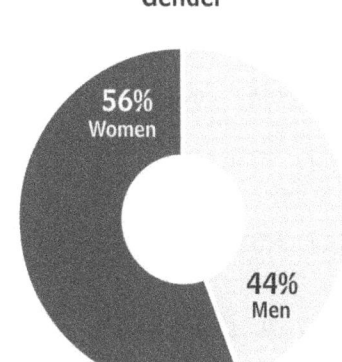

Age

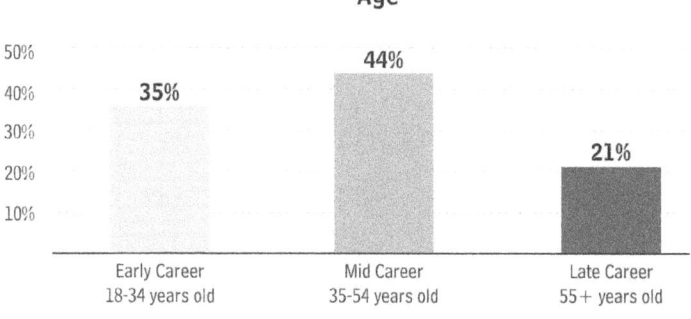

Income

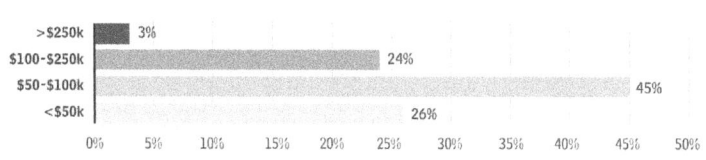

Using these various dimensions, we evaluated employees' feelings and attitudes toward issues such as financial stress, goals and concerns, budgeting and debt, retirement confidence, saving and investing, desire for advice and support, managing risk, and overall satisfaction with company benefits.

Based on the survey results, in the next two chapters, I have highlighted several observations and areas that employers, advisors, and recordkeepers should consider to meet the evolving needs of employees.

FINANCIAL WELLNESS VERSUS FINANCIAL WELL-BEING

The terms *financial wellness* and *financial well-being* are often used interchangeably, but they mean different things, although they are related. Financial wellness is more action-oriented and is the combination of positive steps a person can take to lead a healthier financial life. Financial well-being is more of a holistic, emotional state that focuses on contentment, balance, positivity, and confidence.

I describe financial wellness as process focused (what you do) and financial well-being as outcome focused (how you feel). Financial wellness influences financial well-being. For instance, if you pay off your credit cards every month, you are unlikely to worry about short-term debt. This chart describes some of the differences between financial wellness and financial well-being.

Financial Wellness	Financial Well-Being
Centered on actions	Centered on emotions
Process focused	Outcome focused
The combination of positive steps you take to lead a healthier financial life (what you do), such as:	More holistic and focused on contentment, balance, positivity, and confidence (how you feel), such as:
Having a written financial plan	Do you experience regular financial stress?
Having enough money in emergency savings	Does that stress impact your health, relationships, and/or work quality or attendance?
Paying off credit cards every month	
Saving enough for retirement to meet monthly retirement income needs	Are you worried about debt?
Investing prudently and appropriately	Do you feel like your employer cares about you?
Having appropriate insurance coverages	

Better financial wellness leads to higher financial well-being, which can result in more engaged, productive, and aligned employees. From an employer's perspective, these types of employees achieve better business outcomes and tend to have lower costs, both directly and indirectly.

For instance, in Deloitte's 2019 Global Human Capital Trends, 84 percent of more than ten thousand survey respondents rated improving the employee experience as important to improving productivity. And 28 percent identified it as one of the three most urgent issues facing their organizations in 2019. Furthermore, a 2017 MIT research brief surveying 281 senior executives found that companies delivering top-quartile employee experiences achieve twice the innovation, double the customer satisfaction, and 25 percent greater profitability compared to competitors with bottom-quartile employee experiences.[51]

CHAPTER 22

Gender, Age, and Income Differences (Ps)

GENDER

There were stark differences between men and women based on our survey responses. Women were 27 percent more likely to experience financial stress, 35 percent less confident in making financial decisions, 33 percent less likely to feel confident in managing debt, and 1.9 times less confident in their ability to retire. They were also less likely to have an emergency fund, to have higher levels of short-term and retirement savings, and to feel that their employer cares about them or that their compensation is keeping pace with the cost of living.

Across the board, men expressed higher levels of confidence in making financial decisions. This could be tied to greater levels of saving and lower levels of debt, although a deeper look at the data shows this confidence could be overstated. While retirement was the major goal for both genders, women were more focused on budgeting, debt management, and overall financial planning, while men placed a higher priority on managing investments.

Despite these differences, overall retirement confidence was low for both genders. Only 27 percent of men and 14 percent of women felt confident they will retire on time. A major driver of these confidence issues for both men and women could be the fact that only 26 percent of men and 22 percent of women had a written financial plan.

AGE

Employees identified different priorities and concerns based on age as defined by their career stage.

Early career employees (18–34) experienced the highest levels of financial stress (51 percent) and were most concerned about budgeting and debt management (especially student loan debt), although they expressed confidence in having debt under control and managing things like credit card debt very well. They also were the least confident in managing their own investments (26 percent). Furthermore, they were most open to automatic enrollment, automatic escalation, and target date fund (TDF) investing, which makes sense given that this demographic entered the workforce during a time when more employers had adopted these plan design features.

Midcareer employees (35–55) were in the toughest position, exhibiting the lowest levels of confidence in their ability to make good financial decisions (43 percent), doubting their ability to retire on time (15 percent), and struggling the most with debt (49 percent). They were also most likely to have no emergency savings (33 percent). This may be because they are part of the "sandwich generation" and supporting the financial needs of both children and parents, which detracts from their ability to focus on their own financial priorities.

Late-career employees (55+) were much more likely to focus on issues such as retirement (70 percent) as their highest priority while experiencing the lowest levels of financial stress (32 percent). They were most likely to be adequately insured, to have engaged in some level of estate planning, and to have a written financial plan (32 percent, although this percentage was still low). They also expressed the highest levels of confidence that their employer cares for them and offers competitive benefits.

Employees of all ages worried about running out of money, and they were fearful they weren't saving enough for retirement.

INCOME

As you would expect, financial stress decreased and overall confidence increased with income. The lowest-paid employees exhibited the highest levels of stress (65 percent), debt management issues (67 percent), the lowest levels of short-term and retirement savings, and highest concerns that their compensation wasn't keeping pace with the cost of living (75 percent). Employees making under $50,000 were the most at-risk group.

Every financial measure improved as employees made more money—financial stress and debt decreased, savings and confidence increased, and retirement readiness went up. However, while these measures got better on a relative basis, the overall numbers still suggested that employees of all income levels weren't where they should be.

CHAPTER 23

———

Participant Strategies, Ideas, and Recommendations (Ps)

FINANCIAL STRESS IS REAL AND IMPACTFUL

By every measure, financial stress has a negative impact on people's feelings, perceptions, levels of confidence, and financial preparedness. To illustrate the point, here is a comparison of responses from employees who said they experienced financial stress versus those who did not.

2.9 times more worried about their debt being out of control	51 percent more worried about their debt being out of control
17 times more likely to feel like stress has impacted the quality of their work	56 percent more likely to believe their employer's benefits are less competitive than similar organizations
5 times more likely to be worried about running out of money	33 percent less likely to feel like their employer cares about them
16 times less likely to be saving for retirement	45 percent less likely to feel confident they are taking full advantage of company benefits

THE DESIRE FOR OBJECTIVE AND
PERSONALIZED ADVICE

It's also clear that employees desire (and need) more support and help. Employees across every dimension expressed a preference for unbiased advice based on a fiduciary relationship. And they want this advice to be personalized.

Access to financial planning tools and one-on-one meetings with an independent fiduciary advisor were their highest priorities, especially when they need to make important financial decisions. Traditional methods of financial education (e.g., articles, newsletters, webinars, videos, and group presentations) were much less likely to be viewed as "extremely important" or "very important." Most of the industry has launched financial wellness initiatives that skew toward content and education, especially as it relates to budgeting and debt management, which may signal the current approach is missing the mark.

To use a different metaphor, when a person is sick and visits the doctor, they want that person (who is a trained professional) to provide an accurate diagnosis and prescribe a course of action that improves their health. Most people would see little value in a doctor who just provides them with articles from medical journals or recommends they attend a seminar or workshop where they could become more knowledgeable about medical issues and better able to self-diagnose. And yet, the retirement industry isn't providing enough objective and personalized advice to improve the financial health of employees, the vast majority of whom aren't trained or qualified to do it themselves. Interestingly, few employees use a financial advisor, especially those who are younger and lower paid, people who may not be attractive to the traditional advisor community. So employers have a real opportunity to meet this need for their people.

Employees overwhelmingly seek advice when they "have an important financial decision to make" and want access to an unbiased advisor as a sounding board. One potential strategy is to offer the equivalent of a financial telemedicine service, where employees can get on-demand advice from a qualified and objective advisor like a CERTIFIED FINANCIAL PLANNER™ professional.

IMPORTANCE OF A WRITTEN FINANCIAL PLAN

Some say that a goal without a plan is just a wish. A surprising (though not shocking) fact is that very few employees have a written financial plan. I believe this is a major contributor to high levels of financial stress and low levels of confidence.

Research shows having a financial plan is an important factor for exhibiting financial confidence and achieving financial success.[52] Charles Schwab's 2018 Modern Wealth Index scored one thousand American's between 1 and 100 based on how well they manage their money and investments across four factors:

1. Goal setting and financial planning
2. Saving and investing
3. Staying on track
4. Confidence in reaching financial goals

When Schwab evaluated the top 10 percent of overall performers, they found that 75 percent said they had a written financial plan. However, across the entire survey, only 25 percent of respondents had one.

Those percentages align almost perfectly to our own research from 2019.[53] Only 24 percent of all employees had a written financial plan, and only 36 percent of even the highest-income employees making more than $250,000 had one.

A written financial plan is the best way for any employee to develop a clear understanding of whether they are on track to a successful retirement; gain an accurate assessment of future retirement income needs; understand the sufficiency of their current savings levels; decide whether the investment strategy they have in place is correct; and determine whether they have appropriate insurance coverage and proper estate planning documents, such as a will, powers of attorney, and advanced medical directives. A written plan should also provide a clear set of actionable strategies that can simplify the financial decision-making process and improve overall confidence.

Providing employees with access to robust financial planning tools rather than just lightweight solutions, such as traditional retirement calculators that many recordkeepers offer, would appear to be a step in the right direction. In fact, employees viewed access to financial planning tools as the most valuable resource employers could provide, ranking higher than even access to one-on-one advice.

A better approach would be to provide employees with access to planning tools where they can update their data on a self-service basis and then make a qualified advisor like a CERTIFIED FINANCIAL PLANNER™ professional available to help contextualize results and walk through various what-if scenarios. Another option would be to offer a more robust and structured fixed-fee financial planning solution that employees can pay for themselves (or companies can help subsidize).

LEARNING PATHWAYS AND COMMUNITIES

Given the data, employers should pay special attention to the needs of employees who are underserved or at risk, specifically female and lower-income employees, which are the two groups that exhibited the highest levels of financial stress.

One way companies should consider enhancing the support and resources they offer is by creating curated learning pathways and communities that bring together services, resources, and content in an efficient and organized way and makes it easier for people to engage and learn. Often, plan sponsors, plan providers, and advisors offer access to tremendous (and perhaps overwhelming) amounts of content but fail to make it easy for people to find and use these resources.

For instance, a learning pathway for women could bring together on-demand webinars, e-learning courses, articles, and highly specific one-on-one sessions that focus on areas of concern for women, such as building emergency savings, paying down debt, planning for longevity, and developing a written financial plan. Ongoing engagement could be personalized even further through targeted email automation, notifying each person when new resources become available. Taking this idea one step further, learning communities could be created that bring together employees who have similar goals and common concerns, helping them get specific information and build skills, all while fostering collaborative learning, peer support, mentorship, and so forth. The communities could provide a more personalized experience and connect like-minded employees with one another.

CASE STUDY

At Greenspring Advisors, we've used the data and attitudes of employees to build a participant experience that combines financial wellness with fiduciary advice. We call it (k)larity @ Work. While education and communication can be helpful, we believe that providing one-on-one fiduciary advice to participants is far more effective and engaging. The cornerstone of our solution is on-demand access to a CERTIFIED FINANCIAL PLANNER™ professional as a dedicated point of contact for participants, including access to services in Spanish.

I often describe this like a financial telemedicine service. A few years ago, our firm began offering a telemedicine option that allowed our employees to contact a board-certified, licensed physician that could diagnose illnesses, recommend treatment, and prescribe medications over the telephone or through secure bidirectional video and email. It's been a big hit when our people have basic illnesses since they don't need to make an appointment with their doctor, travel to their office, miss work, etc. Obviously, if someone has a major medical issue like cancer or a torn ACL, a telemedicine service isn't the right solution, and they need to see a specialist. But for things like bronchitis or the flu, where you need a quick diagnosis and prescription, it's a great alternative. Our on-demand CFP professionals are not the right fit when people have major financial issues or need an ongoing comprehensive financial planner. But for many employees that have basic financial issues, questions, and concerns, especially those who don't have access to a qualified advisor, the on-demand approach is a great option.

Participants also have access to our participant advice portal, which includes free access to digital financial planning tools for retirement, budgeting, and debt management, along with hundreds of pieces of educational content, like articles, posts, videos, and webinars. Participants can register for the platform, access all the tools and resources, schedule a one-on-one meeting online, or submit support requests via the site. They can also call our dedicated 800 advice hotline.

5

Ps

Participant Support

SUMMARY

- Overall, 45 percent of employees admit to feeling financial stress.
- Stressed employees are 17 percent more likely to feel like their work quality has suffered, and 33 percent are less likely to feel like their employer cares about them.
- Surveys by Charles Schwab and Greenspring Advisors show that only about 25 percent of employees have a written financial plan.

- Survey your employees to identify feelings, attitudes, and perceptions based on gender, age, and income so you can better target your financial wellness and well-being initiatives to their needs.

- Create learning pathways and communities to make it easier for your employees to engage, learn, and support one another.
- Provide employees with robust digital financial tools and on-demand access to a CERTIFIED FINANCIAL PLAN-NER™ professional.

1. Have you conducted a financial wellness and well-being survey with your employees?
2. Have you implemented a financial wellness program for your employees?
3. Do you provide your participants with on-demand access to a CERTIFIED FINANCIAL PLANNER™ professional for one-on-one meetings?
4. Do your participants have access to robust digital financial planning tools for retirement probability modeling, budgeting, and debt management?
5. Have you created learning pathways to make it easier for your employees to engage and learn?
6. Have you sponsored learning communities that bring together your employees who have similar goals and common concerns to help them get specific information and to build skills while fostering collaborative learning, peer support, mentorship, etc.?

6

Pm

Provider Management

CHAPTER 24

=====

Developing Strong Service Provider Partnerships (Pm)

In *The Merchant of Venice*, William Shakespeare penned the now-famous phrase "All that glitters is not gold." Well, technically, he used the word *glisters*, which was a seventeenth-century synonym for *glitters*, but you get my point.

Having owned a company for fifteen years and having been a retirement plan advisor for nearly that entire time, I've come to realize this adage is often true in both general business and the retirement industry. We all want things to be easy because life and business are complex. And it's tempting to fall victim to the slick sales pitches that come our way every day, especially in the professional services world.

No one in the industry leads with a pitch that says, "I will make all kinds of promises to you about the wonderful proactive service I'll provide, and then once you sign the contract, I'll forget everything we talked about and move on to my next prospect." And yet, that happens time and time again in the retirement industry.

If I've learned anything about business throughout my career, it's never to underestimate the value of good service. On more than one occasion in the early years, I recommended a recordkeeper to a client who did a great job during a finals presentation only to find out the real-world client experience was a lot different than promised. That's why I've learned to develop a reasonable level of professional skepticism.

Given the complexity and administrative requirements of corporate retirement plans, having vendor partners (whether recordkeepers, TPAs, auditors, or advisors) who are knowledgeable, responsive, and proactive is often worth its weight in gold.

One of the other big issues with hiring service providers across the spectrum: it's difficult to get an accurate comparison of fees and services on an apples-to-apples basis. Fees are relatively easy to assess, but quality and value are much more difficult to determine. This is challenging in the current environment, where everyone across the industry looks the same and says the same basic things. To the untrained eye, it's hard to separate fact from fiction.

For example, just about every advisor should talk about things like fiduciary governance and processes, fee benchmarking, an IPS, meeting minutes, vendor management, and employee engagement. But the rubber meets the road post sale. Just because every advisor can talk the talk doesn't mean they are a specialist and can walk the walk. The same is true for recordkeepers and TPAs.

I've never met a company that said, "Having a great 401(k) plan is the key to our business success." Most companies I've encountered throughout my career care about having a solid plan, but it's not what I would call a front-burner business issue. In most cases, the threshold of whether a plan is working depends on whether it's easy to administer and whether anyone is complaining.

As fee compression is impacting the industry, especially in the recordkeeper space, service levels are dropping, response times are increasing, workloads are expanding, less experienced staff are being assigned to relationships, and the overall client experience is suffering. This leads to higher levels of frustration by plan sponsors. In the retirement industry, you get what you pay for.

As a plan sponsor, having a strong team of professionals working together on your plan's behalf makes it much more likely you'll have good service experiences. You will get good, objective advice. Your issues will be identified and resolved more quickly. Your committee meetings will be more consistent and productive. And you won't have to do all the heavy lifting by yourself. You should lean heavily on your vendor partners because that's what you're paying for, what you were promised, and what you deserve. I recommend not only setting reasonable expectations for your vendor partners but also holding them accountable with the expectation that they need to elevate their game.

I think that's been one secret to our success at Greenspring over the years. We not only do a good job holding ourselves accountable and keeping our promises, but we also hold other vendors accountable. I think our clients appreciate that we step up and drive the process. As a plan sponsor, if one of your vendor partners doesn't step up and lead, you need to make sure you fill that role yourself or find someone else who will.

In the next few chapters, I'll provide insights on how you can find the right partners to work with.

CHAPTER 25

─────

What to Look for in a Fiduciary Advisor (Pm)

When looking for a competent retirement plan advisor, I think you want to find a firm that combines substantial real-world experience and expertise as an ERISA fiduciary; knowledge of investment and fiduciary best practices; a comprehensive, process-driven service model; and practical experience in organizing and monitoring investment and fiduciary governance programs for defined contribution plans.

While there's no magic number, I think you should look for a firm that works with at least 100 ERISA plans as either an ERISA 3(21) or 3(38) fiduciary. They should have deep fiduciary governance experience to help you minimize corporate risk and liability, and they should have the technical expertise to consult on administrative, compliance, and regulatory issues.

You want a fiduciary expert and thought leader who develops and uses industry-leading tools and methodologies to assist clients with investment oversight and fiduciary monitoring. You also want a firm that can work closely with plan participants on a fiduciary basis to track and measure key success factors to increase the probability of positive retirement outcomes.

An experienced and specialized firm will essentially serve as the outsourced "chief fiduciary officer" for your retirement plan committee. In this role, they will help your organization implement a consistent approach to fiduciary oversight, with a focus on managing plan risks. And they should have a conflict-free business model and complete independence that aligns their interests with yours so that you receive the maximum level of transparency regarding fees and vendor selection/oversight.

I have listed six specific traits of specialized firms that you can use to help make a well-informed hiring decision:

1. **Business Model**—To ensure proper alignment, I recommend hiring a fee-only registered investment adviser (RIA), which eliminates many compensation-related conflicts of interest that impairs the advice they provide to your plan and your people. The firm should maintain no affiliation to any other firm or product provider, and 100 percent of its revenue should come from its investment and fiduciary advisory services. They shouldn't receive any indirect compensation.

2. **ERISA Specialist**—Understanding the nuances of the retirement industry, third-party providers, ERISA, the Internal Revenue Code, fiduciary matters, retirement plan economics, and investment strategy is not a task for the weary. It requires focus, dedication, and deep knowledge. Advising retirement plan committees and working with ERISA plans should not be a sideline business for your advisor—it should be a major focus and driver of growth. This narrow focus should create advantages for them over competitors who may offer services

to ERISA plans as only one of many lines of business. This unfocused approach is most common in large Wall Street firms, banks, and employee benefits brokers.

3. **Experience and Commitment as a Fiduciary**—The firm should be a true fiduciary partner with significant expertise and experience in fiduciary matters. "Fiduciary" shouldn't simply be a marketing buzzword for them. They should serve as an acknowledged fiduciary in writing at both the plan level and participant level to every ERISA client they work with.

4. **Industry Thought Leader**—The firm should be respected as an industry expert and commentator on matters pertaining to retirement security, fiduciary responsibility, and defined contribution plans. This could take the form of authoring books, writing articles for industry journals, speaking at industry conferences, and being extensively quoted in industry publications.

5. **Certification and Licensing**—Designations such as the Accredited Investment Fiduciary®, the Certified Plan Fiduciary Advisor (CPFA), the Certified Retirement Counselor (CRC), the Chartered Retirement Plan Specialist (CRPS), and the Qualified 401(k) Administrator (QKA) combine education, relevant retirement industry experience, and/or professional development. Other designations like the CERTIFIED FINANCIAL PLANNER™ (CFP®) (if participants receive fiduciary advice) and Chartered Financial Analyst (CFA) for investment expertise are also important. While not an all-inclusive list, these are some of the more rigorous designations and show a commitment to professional development and learning. Just be careful: financial designations are a cottage industry, and some aren't worth the paper they are written on.

6. **Innovation**—You should also look for a firm that helps you skate to where the puck is going by creating tools, resources, and deliverables that put you at the forefront of industry best practices.

Given the highly specialized nature of ERISA plans, here are some additional things you should look for when interviewing prospective advisors. Be sure to pay close attention to how the firm/advisor answers certain questions. For example, if you're seeking services for your company's 401(k) plan, it's important to know how many 401(k) plans a *specific team or advisor* works with rather than the entire firm. If an advisor works at a large firm, they may list thousands of plans at the firm level, but that won't indicate their experience/expertise if they only worked with five plans.

1. **Is the specific team/advisor independent?** You'll want to know if the specific team/advisor has any affiliated organizations or lines of business that could create perceived or actual conflicts of interest and if they have any policies for avoiding them. Also, do they receive any compensation that could impair their objectivity?

2. **What's the overall retirement plan consulting philosophy for the specific team/advisor, and what do they hope to achieve for your plan and your people?** This is a great way to find out what the specific team/advisor stands for and whether their approach will be a good fit for your plan.

3. **How long has the specific team/advisor you'll be working with provided services to defined ERISA plans?** The ability to get results for clients and develop the requisite experience and expertise is accumulated over time. If they are newer to the ERISA space, it's unlikely they have the deep pool of knowledge they need to be effective.

4. **Does the specific team/advisor work only as an ERISA 3(21) and/or 3(38) fiduciary at both the plan level and participant level?** Any team/advisor working with your plan should be able to work in either capacity when providing advice to both your committee and your employees. And they should take this approach with all clients, not just some engagements.

5. **How many ERISA plans does the specific team/advisor work with?** You should look for a team/advisor who works with 100-plus ERISA plans. Find out how many ERISA plans they've won and lost over the past three years to gauge their commitment to the retirement industry and measure which direction their practice is going.

6. **How many staff members of the specific team/advisor work with ERISA plans? How many specialize in these types of plans?** There should be a dedicated team/advisor you will work with at the firm who specializes and focuses on ERISA plans. For instance, an advisor who only works with ERISA plans is likely to have more experience and deeper expertise than an advisor who splits their time between ERISA plans and wealth management clients.

7. **A list of the various services the specific team/advisor provides to defined contribution clients and a description of each.** You should look for references and thorough descriptions of things like fiduciary governance and process, investment selection and monitoring, fee analysis, benchmarking and negotiation, plan design consulting and implementation, vendor management, search and selection, and financial wellness and fiduciary advice, among other things.

8. **What percentage of the specific team's/advisor's revenue do services to ERISA plans represent?** You are looking for a meaningful percentage of overall revenue derived from services to ERISA plans.

9. **What are the total assets under advisement and the number of participants in ERISA plans that the specific team/advisor works with?** Another question to determine if the team/advisor specializes and has achieved critical mass in their ERISA practice.

10. **Does the firm have professional liability coverage for investment advisory services specifically for retirement plans**

regulated by ERISA? You'll want to confirm they have affirmative fiduciary coverage for ERISA-related acts.

II. **Have them provide two to three examples of how they have gone above and beyond to meet the complex challenges of their clients.** Questions like this are excellent for going deeper and reading between the marketing lines. A specialized advisor will have the real-world experience to provide many thorough examples.

To download a more comprehensive sample advisor RFP template with more than forty questions, please visit FiduciaryU.com.

CHAPTER 26

What to Look for in a Recordkeeper/TPA (Pm)

Finding a good recordkeeper and/or third-party administrator (TPA) isn't always easy, but it's essential to the overall health, operation, and compliance of your plan. Before I talk about what to look for, let me start by reviewing the roles and responsibilities of each.

A recordkeeper handles many important administrative duties. For instance, they manage day-to-day operations like processing enrollments, managing and tracking employee investments, implementing automatic features, and processing and tracking any contributions and distributions (e.g., pretax contributions, Roth, employer pretax match, rollovers, loans, hardship withdrawals, etc.). The recordkeeper also produces plan statements for employees and most likely provides the call center and online experience for both employees and the plan sponsor to manage and administer the plan.

A TPA focuses on plan compliance such as preparing the annual

Form 5500, producing and/or managing plan documents, performing annual nondiscrimination testing, helping correct operational failures, and preparing and distributing participant notices. They may also provide plan design consulting for things like eligibility, automatic enrollment, and escalation, and analyzing profit-sharing and/or matching scenarios.

When these functions are handled by the same vendor, it's known as a bundled solution. When these two functions are handled by separate vendors, it's known as an unbundled solution. Both models have strengths and weaknesses, and it's important to understand both so you can make the best decision for your plan, your people, and your company.

The one-stop-shop approach of the bundled strategy can be easier for a plan sponsor to manage, and there are efficiencies gained by keeping these two services under one roof. However, many bundled providers have asset management arms (e.g., Vanguard, Fidelity, T. Rowe Price, etc.) that often look to use their record-keeping platform as a distribution vehicle for their proprietary funds. Although the industry has moved to an "open architecture" approach, these fund companies will jump at promoting their own funds if given the opportunity. As I discussed in the chapter about litigation trends, these proprietary conflicts can cause a lot of problems. That's part of the reason an independent fiduciary advisor can be such a valuable part of the process by enforcing appropriate levels of accountability and objectivity. The bundled approach also rarely works well for plans with complex profit-sharing or matching formulas (like many professional services organizations) such as a cross-tested, profit-sharing plan. Sometimes, a bundled provider will bring in a TPA to do the profit-sharing calculations but continue to do all the other administrative duties. I've also found the bundled approach to be much more common as plans get larger. Most plans I work with are bundled, but there is clearly a place for the unbundled approach.

The unbundled approach can be better if there are greater compliance needs or situations in which a company wishes to define different classes of employees (e.g., owner vs. nonowners) and contribute different profit-sharing amounts to each. This occurs much more in smaller, closely held plans. Good TPAs are very technical and compliance focused.

When shopping for a recordkeeper and/or TPA, there are a lot of details to consider because these vendors play a crucial role in the day-to-day administrative operations of your plan. A poor choice can lead to expensive operational problems and significant, time-consuming administrative headaches. One problem I've seen over the years is a failure for recordkeepers and TPAs to have an open and honest dialogue about roles and responsibilities with clients.

Frequently, I've started working with a plan, and the plan sponsor was convinced that the vendor was doing a terrible job and that we needed to move the plan. My preference is to improve and optimize the plan with the existing vendor(s) unless the relationship is beyond repair. Moving a plan is a lot of work and a big undertaking for everyone involved. It can always be done down the road, but I've found it's usually unnecessary at the outset. Often, the issue stems from the lack of communication between the parties and misaligned expectations, two dilemmas that never lead to good outcomes in business or life.

So the plan sponsor thinks the vendor is taking care of certain things (or doesn't even know what they don't know), and the vendor thinks the plan sponsor is taking care of them or hasn't had the courage to tell them otherwise for fear of conflict or dissatisfaction (this happens often). And then when things break (and things break a lot with retirement plans), everyone gets frustrated and starts pointing fingers. A simple solution is to get everyone in the room (or on the phone) and have a clear conversation about roles and responsibilities. This almost always leads to enlightenment (i.e., aha moments), higher levels of satisfaction and lower levels of frustration, and over time, a much better customer service experience. On many occasions, I've taken this approach. Often, within a year, the plan sponsor says how glad they were they didn't move the plan.

DECLINING SERVICE LEVELS

A current challenge I am seeing with recordkeepers is the decline of service levels. Recordkeeping isn't a very profitable stand-alone business, which is why many of the most well-known retirement vendors have affiliated brokerage, insurance, or asset management/mutual fund arms. In the past, the retirement platform was mainly a vehicle with which to distribute these other high-margin products and services.

It was like the Gillette model, where the razor was inexpensive, and the blades were where all the real money was made. When a recordkeeper was guaranteed many of its proprietary mutual funds would be in a plan, recordkeeping services could be a loss leader. This was especially true when those mutual funds were very profitable, actively managed options with high margins.

This all began to change about ten to twelve years ago and was driven by five primary factors:

1. **The move toward "open architecture" platforms**—In the past, recordkeepers with affiliated insurance and mutual fund com-

panies operated in much more of a "closed architecture" model with things like proprietary fund requirements to guarantee their own products were used. For example, a recordkeeper may have had a 60 percent proprietary requirement, which meant that at least 60 percent of funds in the plan were proprietary, creating conflicts of interest and limiting choice (not a long-term winning strategy). The industry has moved away from this model, and most recordkeepers now offer access to open-architecture platforms in which a plan can get any fund available. Since the number of funds in a plan is limited, the downside of open architecture for recordkeepers with asset management or insurance businesses is the increased probability that competing options will crowd out some or all of its own options. There are still some instances where proprietary requirements show up. This is most common with some recordkeepers who are also insurance companies and require the use of their stable value fund.

2. **The role of the independent fiduciary advisor and retirement specialist**—For a long time, many recordkeepers didn't play very nice in the sandbox with advisors, especially fiduciary advisors. Most plan sponsors used nonfiduciary brokers or went directly to the big recordkeeping firms, who loved the fact that they could control the relationship with little accountability. But as more plan sponsors began to turn to advisors who specialized in ERISA plans and embraced the fiduciary approach, recordkeepers have had to change their practices. In many cases, the fiduciary advisor stepped in to become the most-trusted service provider, bringing a fiduciary-based investment consulting approach and a high level of accountability. Fiduciary advisors have also pushed recordkeepers to move to open-architecture platforms, spurring the move away from proprietary requirements.

3. **The focus on fee benchmarking**—In terms of increased

accountability, fiduciary advisors became the tip of the spear from a fee benchmarking perspective, pushing recordkeepers to be more competitive and renegotiating existing fee structures. Combined with the litigation environment, this has reaped huge amounts of cost savings for plans and participants, often to the tune of tens of thousands, hundreds of thousands, or even millions of dollars per year. But it also means that recordkeepers have seen a major reduction in revenue, hurting profit margins.

4. **The shift in asset flows from active to passive**—Often known as the Vanguard effect, the industry has seen a massive shift in asset flows from high-cost, actively managed funds to low-cost products, like index funds and exchange-traded funds (ETFs). According to Morningstar, at the end of 2017, total assets in US mutual funds and ETFs reached a new record of more than $18 trillion from just over $5.5 trillion nearly a decade earlier.[54] Asset managers have felt pressure to lower the fees for their existing active funds, seeing the average expense ratio for an active equity fund decline from just under 1 percent in 2010 to 0.78 percent in 2017. During the same time, the average active bond fund expense ratio went from about 0.70 percent to 0.57 percent. As Morningstar notes, "From 2014 to the present, the only way to get a positive flow is to offer low-cost funds…We've reached the point where it simply doesn't make sense for a fund company to launch a new fund that isn't in the lowest-fee group."

5. **Technology Capex**—A final factor has been the enormous investments that recordkeepers have had to make in technology and digital transformation to win business and keep up with competitors.

In my experience, this combination of factors has had a significant effect on the recordkeeping industry as it relates to customer experience. To counteract the profitability conundrum, record-keepers are responding in several ways. First, they are forcing plan sponsors to do much more from a self-service perspective, making requests online or via call centers. Second, they are increasing staff workloads, especially the day-to-day contacts who work with plans (e.g., relationship managers or RMs). I heard an unconfirmed rumor that one vendor increased RM workloads from 50 to 150 clients! These increased workloads have resulted in much slower response times, where plan sponsors can wait for a week or more to get an answer that used to take a day. Finally, I am seeing less experienced staff (and less expensive) assigned to clients, which impacts the quality of service and advice.

Now, this isn't to say that no recordkeeper or TPA provides good service to plan sponsors. It just means good ones can be hard to find. And when you find a good one, you want to be careful about moving away just to save a few dollars. Warren Buffett, the world's most famous investor, once said that "price is what you pay; value is what you get." Fees should be competitive and reasonable, but I know I've made the mistake more than once of choosing or recommending the lower-cost option only to find out there was a reason for it. And any up-front cost savings were negated by the time spent resolving poor service, lack of responsiveness, or correcting errors.

Our firm has experienced what I call indirect-fee compression over the last few years. As recordkeeper service levels decline for plan sponsors, someone needs to step in to absorb the additional work or get involved to advocate for the client to get the support they need. That usually winds up being our team, so we devote more resources without being compensated. Many of my colleagues at other advisory firms have had similar experiences.

We work with nearly twenty recordkeepers across our client base, and they all offer comparable products, platforms, and pricing. Some may have a better digital platform or stronger compliance function or technology to integrate and automate the administrative process, but all these differences are minor, and anytime one recordkeeper develops something different, within a short time, their competitors catch up and offer something similar.

One thing that every recordkeeper is pushing is its digital platform and participant experience, which are growing increasingly slick. It's easy for plan sponsors to fall in love with these things because they are tangible and visible. And while having good technology is important and can support the client experience, it has become table stakes for every recordkeeper to compete.

In Greek mythology, the Sirens were dangerous creatures who used their enchanting voices to lure sailors to shipwreck and death on the rocky coasts of nearby islands. In *The Odyssey*, Odysseus wanted to hear the Sirens' music. He made his sailors put beeswax in their ears and tie him to the forward mast of the ship. He told the men to keep him tied to the mast no matter how much he begged. When he heard the Sirens' song, he ordered the sailors to untie him, but they obeyed his earlier request and only bound him tighter.

Luckily for Odysseus and his men, he had the foresight to take precautions because he knew his weaknesses. It's a lesson you would be wise to follow. Do not become so married to the digital experience that you lose sight of the most important thing recordkeepers can deliver—a great, responsive client service experience. Recordkeepers won't tell you this, but a very small percentage of participants regularly use the digital experience the way it was intended. Most people simply log in to check their balance and see how their investments have performed. It's tempting to overweigh the importance of digital bells and whistles, but there are many elements that are far more important to drive successful outcomes for both participants and plan sponsors.

So let me share a few things that I look for in recordkeepers and TPAs. I have found these characteristics correlate to a good experience for my clients. The main difference in client experience and satisfaction comes down to the quality of the people assigned to the account. In my opinion, the most important thing to look for is a knowledgeable, proactive, and responsive service team. This starts with a good conversion specialist or team, especially a strong transition manager who can lead the process, manage the timeline, and make sure all required activities and action items are being completed. Getting things set up correctly on the front end is imperative and can minimize the amount of cleanup that needs to happen post conversion. And having good, clean data is essential and perhaps the most important element.

A conversion team may include members like a document specialist, data specialist, compliance/technical specialist, and a communications lead. When we find good conversion teams, we request they are assigned to all our conversions to foster continuity, teamwork, and execution. Since these specialists will roll off the project post conversion, it's ideal to have whoever will be your ongoing contact(s) involved in the conversion. This is usually the RM, and I have found this to be really helpful to creating a good ongoing experience because there's a level of familiarity they have right from the outset. Not all recordkeepers will provide these resources during the conversion process, but always ask.

Next, a strong day-to-day team is essential. Some recordkeepers assign a single point of contact, while others assign multiple team members. Both can work well. For larger plans, there's normally a day-to-day administrative contact and a strategic account manager or RM. Sometimes there may also be a dedicated communications consultant and/or education consultant. The day-to-day contact plays an important role in making sure the administrative and operational tasks are being completed. They should be task- and detail-oriented and knowledgeable about the recordkeeper's internal systems.

But for my money, the strategic account manager, or RM, is the most important cog in the wheel. A good RM is part quarterback and part advocate for the plan sponsor to ensure they're getting all the resources and support the recordkeeper provides. They can run point and play traffic cop to route requests to the proper internal resource or team, advocating for the plan sponsor along the way. A good RM should be an excellent communicator and have good project management and organizational skills. They should also have a strong customer-focused orientation and promptly respond to your needs and requests.

If you're having issues with your service team, don't be afraid to be vocal about it and request different people. Winning new retirement plans is hard (only about 10 percent of plans switch vendors each year), and recordkeepers don't want to lose revenue. To get better customer service, I've always found the squeaky wheel gets the oil. Be realistic but also demanding. This is one area where a great fiduciary advisor can help. We spend a lot of time fighting for our clients and putting pressure on recordkeepers to keep their promises and step up their game. We also tend to get the best resources assigned to our clients because of the number of plans we oversee at many of these vendors.

Here are some key questions you will want to ask prospective recordkeepers and TPAs during the sales process:

- What services do they offer? What services don't they offer? What services are outsourced?
- What responsibilities will the vendor be responsible for, and what will you be responsible for?
- Which services are included in the base fee, and which services are extra?
- Are there any other situations where additional fees will surface?
- What other products or services will the vendor use to derive revenue from your plan?
- What resources, services, and/or tools are available to streamline the administrative process (e.g., 360 payroll integration, mailings, etc.)?
- When a mistake occurs, who is on the hook to fix it and pay for it if there's a cost involved?
- What's the maximum number of conversions their conversion team is assigned to at one time?
- How many people are assigned to your account on a day-to-day basis, and what are their roles/responsibilities? What's the client load for each of these people?

One last thing I want to address is some of the new tactics I'm seeing recordkeepers implement to enhance profitability or increase "enterprise revenue." The first tactic is trying to entice plan sponsors to use proprietary TDFs and/or stable value products by offering fee concessions for including these products. For instance, a recordkeeper will offer lower recordkeeping pricing if the plan sponsor selects their TDF series and commits to a TDF conversion. They know the odds are good that at least 60 to 80 percent of the assets will stay in these funds, creating asset management fees and greater profitability, to say nothing of the fiduciary obligations of TDF selection. Pay attention to this because you can save money on recordkeeping fees but offset any savings by increasing the overall cost of the plan through higher investment management fees. The best way to assess the true cost of recordkeeping is always to get the recordkeeper to quote assuming zero proprietary options.

The second tactic is offering lower recordkeeping pricing if the plan sponsor makes the recordkeeper's proprietary advice solutions available to participants like managed accounts. Either way, it's always smart to exercise a bit of professional skepticism and identify where there might be a misalignment of incentives.

To download a checklist of additional questions to ask your prospective recordkeeper/TPA, please visit FiduciaryU.com.

CHAPTER 27

===

What to Look for in a
Plan Auditor (Pm)

ERISA requires annual audits of plan financial statements by an independent qualified public accountant of plans subject to its provisions. This requirement generally applies to large plans, which are plans with one hundred or more eligible participants on the *first day of the plan year*.

Eligible participants include all current employees eligible to participate in the plan, even those who are not actively contributing. Eligible participants also include terminated participants with an account balance. For purposes of this count, the only day of the year that matters is the first day of each plan year.

While one hundred eligible participants are the magic number that distinguishes large plans from small plans, there is an exception called the 80/120 rule that allows a plan the option to skip the audit requirement. This rule allows plans with between 80 and 120 participants, as of the first day of the plan year, to file the Form 5500 in the same category (large plan or small plan) as indicated on the prior year Form 5500 filing.

For example, if a plan had 110 eligible participants on January 1, 2019, but filed as a small plan on the Form 5500 in 2018, they would be able to file as a small plan in 2019 because they had fewer than 120 eligible participants on the first day of the plan year. But if the plan had 121 eligible participants on January 1, 2019, it would have to file as a large plan on the Form 5500 and be subject to the audit requirement. I've never seen a plan that had the option of avoiding the audit opt for it, but I am sure it has happened. Once the plan drops below one hundred eligible participants on the first day of the plan year, it can file as a small plan and avoid the audit.

A plan files as a small plan by using Schedule I of the Form 5500 and files as a large plan using Schedule H. If your plan is eligible to take advantage of the 80/120 rule, use Schedule I to avoid the audit requirement because audits are always required if you file using Schedule H.

Many plan sponsors have made great strides in hiring record-keepers, TPAs, and specialized retirement plan advisors. However, hiring a specialized employee benefit plan (EBP) auditor is still an afterthought most times because there isn't much of a perceived added value for these audits. It's viewed as just an additional expense the government imposes on your company once you reach a certain size.

I've found there are three main reasons that CPA firms who don't specialize in these types of audits do them:

1. **The client asked them to**—Most professional services firms are in the business of helping clients when asked to do so.

2. **To protect an existing client relationship**—These audits are often included in the larger tax/audit engagement. The last thing a CPA firm wants to do is open themselves up to the risk that a competitor takes a small piece of the action by doing the plan audit in year one and then pitches on the entire engagement in year two.

3. **It's a great way to train new or associate-level staff**—Many firms that don't have specialized EBP teams use these audits as summer work to train junior staff and keep the internal cost low because these audits aren't big revenue generators.

While most CPA firms will say they *can* conduct an EBP audit (which may be true), whether they have the specialized expertise and experience may be a different story. EBP audits differ from most audits because they contain two components: the financial statement audit and compliance. Most auditors are familiar with the financial statement component, but compliance includes the interplay of both the DOL and IRS rules and regulations, which are complex. Most auditors that conduct few EBP audits might not be as familiar with them. An auditor also needs to understand the nature of plan operations that affect every plan and can add to the complexity of an EBP audit.

The DOL views a good quality audit as necessary to "help protect the assets and the financial integrity of your employee benefit plan and provide the plan administrator with information to help ensure that the necessary funds will be available to pay retirement, health and other promised benefits."[55]

The DOL holds plan sponsors responsible to ensure that plan financial statements are properly audited in accordance with generally accepted auditing standards (GAAS), and substandard audit work can result in civil penalties against the plan sponsor by the DOL.

Unfortunately, the DOL has expressed a high level of concern about the audit quality of employee benefit plans and many of the CPA firms who perform these audits. In 2015, the DOL released a report that assessed the quality of audit work by CPAs regarding employee benefit plan audits for the 2011 filing year. The Employee Benefits Security Administration (EBSA) conducted the study and found:

- **Major deficiencies**—39 percent of the audits contained major deficiencies regarding one or more relevant GAAS requirements which would lead to rejection of a Form 5500 filing, putting $653 billion and 22.5 million participants and beneficiaries at risk.
- **The link between experience and quality**—CPAs who performed the fewest number of EBP audits each year had a 76 percent deficiency rate as compared to firms performing the most plan audits (>100) which had a deficiency rate of only 12 percent.
- **Acceptable peer reviews do not equate to higher work quality**—CPAs who performed deficient audits often received acceptable peer review reports.
- **Specialized training improves quality**—CPA firms that were members of the American Institute of Certified Public Accountants' (AICPA's) Employee Benefit Plan Audit Quality Center (EBAQC) tended to produce audits that had the fewest audit deficiencies. The center is a voluntary membership organization that helps to educate, train, and support firms that specialize in EBP audits.[56]

Because of the study, EBSA made many recommendations, including an initiative to target CPA firms with smaller EBP audit practices that audited plans with large amounts of plan assets, and CPA firms that conducted twenty-five to ninety-nine plan audits, for a 42 percent deficiency rate for these firms while auditing substantial amounts of plan assets.

Hiring the right auditor requires consideration of licensing and independence rules and the auditor's experience and professional development, including specific EBP audit experience and continuing professional education.

Given the specialized field of EBP audits, here are some things you should look for when considering EBP auditors:

1. **Is the firm certified and independent?** An auditor must be licensed or certified as a public accountant with a state regulatory authority and is required to be independent to render an objective opinion on the plan's financial statements.
2. **How many plan audits does the firm perform?** Given the evidence of deficiency rates, look for a firm that conducts more than one hundred EBP audits. Ask how many plans they've audited in the last twelve to twenty-four months.
3. **How many staff members work on EBP audits? How many specialize in these types of audits?** There should be a dedicated team within the firm that only specializes and focuses on EBP audits.
4. **What type of EBP-specific training and continuing education does the firm provide and how does the firm keep current with changes in laws and regulations?** Ask about EBP-specific training programs they provide/require and what percentage of the CPE credits obtained by the supervisors, managers, and partners of the audit team is EBP-specific.
5. **Have the firm explain the audit process, including planning, fieldwork, and completion.** Firms that are experienced should be able to explain the audit process in a clear and simple manner.

6. **Is the firm a member of the AICPA Employee Benefit Plan Audit Quality Center (EBPAQC)?** The DOL found that EBPAQC members had far fewer deficiencies in plan audits than those who are not members, so make sure the firm is a member.

7. **Does the firm specialize in particular areas of EBP audits, such as employee stock ownership plans (ESOPs), health and welfare plans, or defined benefit pension plans?** If your company has these types of plans, you will want to make sure the auditor has the right level of knowledge and experience to handle the engagement.

8. **Can the firm provide credible references from EBP clients?** Ask for references from EBP clients who you can speak with.

9. **Have the firm's plan audits undergone an AICPA peer review or review by the Public Company Accounting Oversight Board (PCAOB) or the DOL?** AICPA firms are required to have their practice reviewed by an outside CPA firm every three years. Ask how many EBP audits were selected in the review process and the outcome of the reviews. Also, ask to see the peer review report letter and whether the firm received a rating of "pass" and the results of any DOL reviews that have been completed and if they received a clean "no change" letter. Finally, if your company is public and files a Form 11-K with the SEC, the auditor is subject to inspection by the PCAOB, so ask to see the public portion of that report.

10. **Does the firm have experience in dealing with your recordkeeper and/or a TPA?** A high level of familiarity can help ensure the audit process runs more smoothly.

11. **What other industry specialists does the firm have relationships with?** A good firm will have established professional relationships with attorneys, actuaries, TPAs, and advisors/consultants throughout the industry.

To download a more comprehensive sample auditor RFP template with nearly twenty-five questions, please visit FiduciaryU.com.

CASE STUDY

Conducting a formal full-scope process requires a lot of work, time, and effort. As I discussed in chapter 15, it need not be done every year, but I recommend doing it every three to five years, or when poor service levels are being delivered and a change is necessary.

To see this in action, let me share our firm's proprietary methodology for conducting an effective recordkeeper RFP. This is something we do as part of our service model for our retainer clients or for companies as a project-based consulting engagement. While this is recordkeeper-specific, you can modify it for an advisor or auditor search.

The first step is to have each member of the committee take a short provider capabilities survey, which only takes one to two minutes. Each person ranks your plan's needs in order of individual priority based on the following eight criteria:

1. **Total Cost**—Overall cost of recordkeeping services for the value received.
2. **Participant Support**—Resources available to provide educational and/or advisory support for participants (e.g., webinars, collateral, in-person group education, enrollment support, one-to-one fiduciary advice, etc.).
3. **Access to Broad Array of Investments**—Having access to an open-architecture investment platform where there are no fund restrictions or proprietary requirements.
4. **Technology (Participant and Plan Sponsor)**—Participant

and plan sponsor websites, retirement planning tools, mobile application support, and reporting/data analytics capabilities.

5. **Strength of Service Team**—Having a capable, knowledgeable, and responsive service team to assist with plan administration.

6. **Administrative Support**—The resources, tools, and capabilities to help outsource and automate processes associated with plan administration (e.g., sending notices, data integration, compliance services, etc.).

7. **Communications Capabilities**—The ability to customize, brand, and deliver targeted communications pieces to employees as a whole and by segment (e.g., location, age demographic, etc.).

8. **Brand Recognition**—Name recognition of the vendor from an employee perception standpoint.

Although the eight criteria are the same for each search, it customizes the level of priority for each to the individual plan sponsor based on the unique responses by committee members through the online survey process. Once you gather the survey responses, analyze the data, and develop a weighted scoring system that ranks the eight key areas in order of priority. This approach avoids a one-size-fits-all strategy and ensures the process aligns with the unique goals and needs of your specific plan.

Next, you'll want to develop a plan profile that includes key priorities as well as background information about your plan, such as assets, number of accounts (active and terminated with a balance), annual cash flow history, loan information, plan design features (e.g., automatic enrollment, escalation, etc.), employer contribution formula(s), and number of payroll feeds. Once this plan profile is complete, you can send it to prospective bidders and request a formal proposal and a required revenue quote for recordkeeping/administration services, assuming a zero-revenue sharing fund lineup. The benefit of this approach is that it isolates the true cost of recordkeeping services on an apples-to-apples basis among competing bidders. It also identifies potential conflicts of interest and avoids the possibility that vendors can manipulate or misrepresent the true cost of their services by using proprietary products or through indirect compensation arrangements. You should also request both a fixed, per-participant fee and an asset-based fee as part of the initial bid.

Once you receive all proposals and initial bids, your committee should review the information and decide which vendors to select as finalists (three to four is sufficient, depending on whether the incumbent is rebidding) and select date(s) for presentations to the committee to take place. If possible, schedule all the presentations on a single day.

Next, contact each bidder and inform them if they are a finalist. Out of professional courtesy, I suggest offering a debrief call with any vendors who weren't selected to answer questions or tell them why they weren't chosen.

For the finalists, I recommend scheduling a prefinals conference call/meeting to answer questions they may have to prepare for their finals presentation, and I would encourage them to focus their pitch on the areas that are the highest priority to your company. Your goal is to provide each finalist with the information they need to help them make their best presentation in the time allotted. You should also coordinate the scheduling process and time slot for each vendor. I find these prefinals calls to be valuable and appreciated by vendors.

As part of the finals process, consider putting together a binder of information for each committee member that includes an agenda, background information about each vendor, and a scoring worksheet so committee members can grade each vendor on the eight criteria of priority. You will also want to facilitate each presentation to make sure each vendor stays on track.

After the last presentation, I suggest setting aside an additional sixty to ninety minutes with the committee to discuss each one. Make sure to stack rank each vendor's performance in the eight key areas (based on each member's perspective) to derive an overall weighted score for each one. In almost every case, this review of both quantitative and qualitative factors yields a decision at this point.

As a final step, contact the chosen vendor (but not the other finalists) and request a best and final offer, negotiating the final pricing and service terms and asking for a letter of intent. Once the letter of intent is signed, you can tell the remaining finalists they were not selected and schedule a debrief conference call to discuss their questions. I find the process takes two to three months from start to finish.

Feedback from our clients shows they've found the process thorough, enlightening, and beneficial to gain enhanced services and lower fees, among other things. They also like that our firm does most of the heavy lifting so that each member only needs to fill out the survey and attend the finals presentations. We've also gotten great feedback from vendors (including those who are not selected) in terms of how organized, efficient, and comprehensive the process runs.

6

Pm

Provider Management

SUMMARY

- According to DOL's audit-quality analysis, 39 percent of the audits contained major deficiencies regarding one or more relevant GAAS requirements.
- CPAs who performed the fewest number of employee benefit plan audits each year had a 76 percent deficiency rate.
- Audit firms that performed the most plan audits (>100) had a deficiency rate of only 12 percent.

- Conduct a limited or full-scope RFP for your service providers every three to five years or when poor service levels are being delivered and a change is necessary.

- Make sure your advisor is an ERISA specialist and works with more than one hundred plans.
- Ask prospective advisors questions related to the *specific team or advisor* you will be working with rather than the entire firm to assess their experience/expertise.
- Determine whether to use bundled or unbundled recordkeeping and administration services.
- Request that your recordkeeper includes your ongoing account team (e.g., RM and day-to-day contact) to be part of the conversion process.
- Pay special attention to recordkeepers that offer lower recordkeeping pricing for proprietary options (e.g., TDFs or stable value) that could offset any cost savings by increasing the overall cost of the plan through higher investment management fees.
- Hire an auditor that audits more than one hundred plans.
- Hire an auditor that is a member of the AICPA Employee Benefit Plan Audit Quality Center (EBPAQC).

1. Do you have an ERISA 3(21) or 3(38) advisor for your plan?
2. Do they acknowledge fiduciary status at the plan level *and* participant level?
3. Does your advisor work with more than one hundred plans?
4. Are you experiencing satisfactory service levels from your recordkeeper?
5. If not, do you need to request a new RM or day-to-day contact?
6. Have you conducted an advisor RFP in the last three to five years?
7. Have you conducted a recordkeeper RFP in the last three to five years?
8. Do you have a dedicated EBP team that audits more than one hundred plans?
9. Is your auditor a member of the AICPA Employee Benefit Plan Audit Quality Center (EBPAQC)?
10. Do you have documentation to support the selection of each service provider?

CHAPTER 28

The Fiduciary of
the Future

Yogi Berra was an eighteen-time all-star and ten-time World Series Champion for the New York Yankees in the 1940s, 1950s, and 1960s. He had a career batting average of .285, hit 358 home runs, and had 1,430 runs batted in. He is one of only six players to win the American League Most Value Player Award on three separate occasions and was elected to the Baseball Hall of Fame in 1972. Needless to say, he was a pretty talented and well-known ballplayer.

But Yogi is most remembered for his ability to turn a phrase, even more so than his skill at swinging a bat. One of my favorite Yogi quotes is, "It's tough to make predictions, especially about the future."

In 2014, I wrote an op-ed for the "Voice" section of *PLANSPONSOR* magazine that I titled "A Call to Action." I've included an excerpt here:

It's time that we in the retirement collective (i.e., both plan sponsors and members of the retirement industry) ask ourselves an honest question. Are we serious about having corporate retirement programs that help employees retire successfully? If the answer to that question is yes, and we actually mean it, then we have to change what we're doing. We have to change our way of thinking and stop accepting mediocrity. We have to be purpose-filled and mission-driven. What if having a great retirement program became a key business driver and top priority for every company? What if helping employees achieve a fully funded retirement became just as important as increasing shareholder value? What if companies stopped pretending that a 3 percent contribution would actually move the needle for employees and decided to be more generous? What if corporate retirement funding was viewed as an investment in human capital instead of an expense on a financial statement? What if we started to tell the truth to employees about how much they actually needed to save? What would that look like? How would employees feel if they knew a core value of their employer was to help them achieve a comfortable retirement? Better yet, how would these workers respond? Would they be more loyal? More productive? More appreciative? Or more committed to the success of your company?

I certainly don't profess the ability to tell the future, but I do want to share several ideas about how the fiduciary landscape could change over the next five to ten years. During the coming years, I expect the focus of fiduciaries to evolve from a primary focus on plan governance and due diligence (often described as "funds, fees, and fiduciary") to delivering successful participant outcomes and retirement readiness, enhanced by personalized solutions, digital experiences, and technological advancements.

I hope these ideas will cast a new vision for the fiduciaries of today to stay at the forefront of the trends of tomorrow.

INCREASED COMPANY GENEROSITY

In the first century, the Apostle Peter wrote, "Above all, love each other deeply, because love covers over a multitude of sins."[57] When it comes to financial planning, a person's savings rate covers a multitude of financial sins. Simply put, it's the single most important driver of retirement success for your employees. Although it's not ideal, they can recover from high fees and even mediocre investment options. But no one can invest their way out of a savings deficit.

A common rule of thumb is that employees should be saving a minimum of 10 percent of their income each year, including their own contributions and employer contributions. In fact, I referenced this idea in chapter 6 as part of the 90-10-90 rule. But remember, 10 percent should be the floor, not the ceiling. Realistically, most employees should probably be saving between 15 to 25 percent to counteract increases in the cost of living and expanding life expectancies. But there's no way employees can get to these types of savings levels without significantly more help from their employers.

Retirement benefits are taking a more prominent role in the eyes of employees. A 2014 survey by Fidelity Investments found that 43 percent of workers said they would accept lower pay for a higher 401(k) match.[58] Glassdoor, one of the world's largest job and recruiting sites, found that 80 percent of employees prefer new or additional benefits to a pay increase.[59] Millennials were even more likely to hold this opinion, with 90 percent stating this preference. The common 3 percent match is simply not enough for any company that really cares about the financial well-being of its employees and is committed to their success.

In 2018, Visa changed its matching formula to 200 percent of employee contributions up to 5 percent, for a maximum match of 10 percent.[60] Visa employees who save at least 5 percent capture the full match and achieve a savings of 15 percent. Visa also increased the automatic enrollment default percentage to 5 percent. If you factor in automatic escalation increases, it's possible (even likely) employees at Visa can reach a threshold of 20 percent within five years of hire. The company explained the move by saying, "With the additional 401(k) match, Visa's US employees will enjoy a sustained benefit, *consistent with the role they will play in building our business.*"[61]

I applaud Visa for its commitment to its employees and tying retirement benefits to its growth strategy. What type of goodwill do you think this creates with Visa employees or for prospective hires versus its competition? As the battle for recruiting and retaining top talent continues to intensify, I believe the companies who thrive will be the ones who make retirement funding a core aspect of its human capital strategy.

NEW SUCCESS OBJECTIVES

John Doerr is an American investor and venture capitalist at Kleiner Perkins, best known for his early stage investments in companies like Google and Amazon. Early in his career, he worked at Intel for Andy Grove, who taught him about an objectives-based management approach he named Objectives and Key Results, or OKRs. In his book *Measure What Matters*, Doerr defines OKRs as a collaborative goal-setting tool used by teams and individuals to set challenging, ambitious goals with measurable results. OKRs are how you track progress, create alignment, and encourage engagement around measurable goals.

In 1999, Doerr introduced this philosophy to Google co-founders

Larry Page and Sergey Brin, which revolutionized how Google managed its business and helped create the foundation for its incredible success. Hundreds, if not thousands, of companies around the world have implemented the OKR system as a result (including our team at Greenspring Advisors).

The key with OKRs is that they are ambitious and should feel somewhat uncomfortable. As Google describes it, the company

> often sets goals that are just beyond the threshold of what seems possible, sometimes referred to as "stretch goals." Creating unachievable goals is tricky as it could be seen as setting a team up for failure. However, more often than not, such goals can tend to attract the best people and create the most exciting work environments. Moreover, when aiming high, even failed goals tend to result in substantial advancements…Such stretch goals are the building blocks for remarkable achievements in the long term, or "moonshots."[62]

Most current retirement plan success measures like participation rates, deferral rates, investment diversification, and account balances are, at best, point-in-time calculations or key performance indicators (KPIs) of existing states. But how many retirement plan committees set formal success objectives and manage toward these outcomes? I believe the fiduciaries of tomorrow will need to adopt an OKR-type approach and focus on big-picture goals and targets that are designed to push committees forward if they are serious about driving successful retirement outcomes for their participants.

Here's an example of what one OKR could look like for a forward-thinking committee. Let's assume a plan currently has a 75 percent participation rate, a matching contribution of 3 percent, and an average total savings rate of 8.5 percent. The committee could set the following OKR.

Objective: Within three years, we will attract and retain top talent by offering the most generous and productive retirement benefit within our industry.

- **Key Result #1:** Increase our matching contribution from 3 percent to 10 percent.
- **Key Result #2:** Increase the average total savings rate from 8.5 percent to 17 percent.
- **Key Result #3:** 100 percent of our employees receive the full match.

The committee could then determine which compensation and plan design strategies to adopt to drive these types of outcomes. For example, if the goal is to increase the matching contribution percentage, it's likely to require some hard financial decisions for the company and the need for tradeoffs and prioritization. Maybe the company identifies cost-saving measures in another area of the business that can be redeployed toward a higher investment in retirement for employees if this becomes the priority. Or given the previously cited employee survey data from Fidelity and Glassdoor, the company may decide to rethink its compensation methodology and reduce cash compensation (or bonuses) to fund additional retirement contributions. My point is that once objectives and key results like this are identified and committed to, creative solutions can be developed to drive toward these outcomes.

And one of the keys to success with OKRs is to make them public so that everyone in the organization can see them, creating transparency and accountability. So imagine if the committee shared its OKRs with all employees, setting audacious goals that ambitiously redefine what success looks like for its retirement committee, and creating a metaphorical North Star for the company's commitment to retirement success. Now, that's an idea worth thinking about. How many retirement committees do you think operate this way today? Based on my experience, not many. And I am speaking to myself and the work I do with my own clients. But, hey, this is my vision for the future, and I'm dreaming a little!

If you're interested in learning more about goal setting and OKRs, whether for your retirement plan or your company, I'd encourage you to visit John Doerr's website (WhatMatters.com) or Google's re:Work website (reWork.withGoogle.com).

HARNESSING THE POWER OF BEHAVIORAL ECONOMICS

In chapters 6 through 9, I highlighted certain elements of behavioral economics and how automatic plan design can lead to better outcomes for participants. But I believe the retirement industry has just started to scratch the surface of how behavioral economics can be harnessed to help participants succeed financially.

In my experience, everything about financial planning comes down to behavior. Unfortunately, most people's brains are wired in a way that sabotages their finances. Traditional economics assumes that people make decisions by gathering all relevant data, processing that information in a rational, unemotional, and self-controlled way, and then arriving at the optimal choice for themselves. It's an elegant theory.

However, behavioral economics challenges those traditional assumptions. In the real world, people make decisions based on incomplete information, are influenced by emotions and cognitive biases that impair their ability to make good choices, and undermine their long-term best interests. People procrastinate, suffer from indecision, take uncalculated risks, give in to desires, and deceive themselves. The result is a destructive disconnect between knowledge and behavior. It's the reason that otherwise intelligent people often make foolish choices. As Dan Ariely said, not only are people irrational; they are *predictably* irrational.

To better understand how participants think and make decisions, I believe the most successful plan fiduciaries of the future will need to become well versed in behavioral finance research and theories. This could include concepts like choice architecture and overload, decision fatigue, myopia, inertia, priming, nudges, mental accounting, cognitive dissonance, social norms, framing, zero price effect, default bias, hindsight bias, anchoring, decoy effect, confirmation bias, and the endowment effect, to name just a few.

Once understood, plan fiduciaries will be better prepared to analyze, design, implement, and test the solutions, programs, communications, and services they make available to their people. For decades, marketers have known how to influence and shape consumer behavior. It's time for plan fiduciaries to start thinking more like marketers. By using insights from behavioral economics, fiduciaries will know exactly how small changes can influence the way people react and design an environment that reinforces more responsible choices and actions.

PERSONALIZED PARTICIPANT SOLUTIONS

In the coming years, I expect the personalization capabilities of financial tools and digital experiences to improve dramatically through the combination of applied behavioral finance and artificial intelligence (AI).

By using more (and better) data to uncover insights about participants, recordkeepers, advisors, and fintech companies will deliver goals-based financial planning and investing solutions that leverage the power of AI technologies, like rules-based algorithms, machine learning (ML), and natural-language processing (NLP).

For instance, chatbots and voice services like Alexa will be able to answer typical questions participants may have about various financial issues, helping them find relevant information more quickly and make better decisions. Automated nudges and messages will be personalized, such as automatically notifying participants who are not contributing enough to get the full company match and providing a link to a webpage where they increase their contribution rate with the click of a button. There will be algorithms and rules that help participants determine the next best step in their financial journey through the integration of things like health savings accounts (HSAs), student loan repayment solutions, 529 plans, or emergency savings accounts.

New investment solutions like dynamic qualified default investment alternatives (QDIAs) will emerge and increase in popularity as well. For example, new default investment solutions may start with TDFs early in a participant's career but transition to managed accounts upon various predefined triggers, such as reaching a certain age, account balance, income, or other factors. And instead of a one-size-fits-all approach, these managed account solutions will be able to incorporate additional data points about participants that may factor into customized portfolio design and decumulation strategies.

These are just a few of the basic applications we are likely to see develop that will automate and personalize retirement planning and turn insights into actions. As technology continues to evolve, the possibilities are endless.

AUTOMATION, BIG DATA, AND DECISION SUPPORT TOOLS

AUTOMATION

Like the emerging improvements in digital participant experiences, technology and digitization hold huge promise for helping plan sponsors manage the fiduciary process and administrative aspects of retirement plans.

For plan sponsors, the use of technology can significantly enhance the successful operation and accuracy of plans through the use of automation. This is crucial because operational missteps and mistakes are common and can be expensive to fix, posing a far greater financial risk than the probability of fiduciary breaches. The Employee Benefits Security Administration (EBSA) of the DOL is responsible for regulating and enforcing DOL regulations regarding retirement plans, including administration requirements of a retirement plan. As I highlighted in chapter 3, the consequences for plan failures can be expensive, including audits, penalties, and correction processes.

The foundation of successful retirement plan administration starts with accurate payroll data. Maintaining accuracy between the plan and the payroll system requires sharing and synchronizing huge amounts of information that needs to be up to date. This includes name and address, compensation, employment status, plan deferral rates, investment allocation, loan data, marital status, and other data. In addition, compliance testing results rely on accurate employee census and historical contribution data.

Many recordkeepers currently offer at least some basic level of automation and functionality, but there is typically a lot of manual intervention still involved. In the future, comprehensive automation will be far more integrated between the retirement plan and payroll system. Data will flow bidirectionally and seamlessly between systems, synchronizing the information, contributions, and money transfers without the need for manual oversight.

Quality assurance processes will profile data to discover and flag inconsistencies and other anomalies, as well as perform cleansing activities to improve the data quality and reconciliation. And sophisticated, intelligent programming interfaces will calculate and apply preset conditions to manage certain processes, such as contribution processing, loan administration, enrollment and eligibility, and census information. Intelligent automation will streamline complex and time-consuming repetitive processes and reduce costs and risks, while freeing internal resources to focus on higher value activities and responsibilities.

BIG DATA AND DECISION-SUPPORT TOOLS

Like many other industries, retirement plan service providers are leveraging big data to gain insights into participant savings behavior, while providing plan fiduciaries with powerful new tools to visualize, analyze, and act upon this data.

Improved data visualization tools and techniques will be another area where big data can help fiduciaries make better forecasting decisions about the potential impact of plan design changes at both the plan and participant level. For instance, plan fiduciaries will be able to see how things like implementing or changing match formulas, increasing automatic enrollment or automatic escalation rates, or reducing access to loans will impact projected participant outcomes and plan costs.

Finally, the increasing amount of data and analysis tools will provide more robust, real-time benchmarking solutions, enhancing due diligence capabilities for plan fiduciaries.

One area that has accelerated in the retirement industry is record-keeper consolidation to drive scale. In the next five to ten years, I expect there will be fewer recordkeepers who can compete at scale. I think it's likely that the pace of this M&A activity will increase, primarily driven by the need for capital investment requirements in technology.

DATA PRIVACY

However, a major issue surrounding the use of big data is the concern over privacy. Many large recordkeepers and asset gatherers are mining participant data to find opportunities for cross-selling other financial products and services. This is especially relevant in the current era of declining recordkeeping margins and the move away from proprietary products as discussed in chapter 26.

There is an emerging focus on retirement plan data by both plaintiffs and litigators, as evidenced by Vanderbilt University's $14.5 million settlement regarding claims involving the university's 403(b) plan.[63] The lawsuit originally focused on excessive fees, but plaintiffs subsequently filed an amended complaint accusing the university of failing to protect plan data by allowing their service providers to market products and services to plan participants. As part of the nonmonetary terms of the settlement, the plan fiduciaries agreed to prohibit current and future recordkeepers from using participant data acquired in the course of providing services to cross-sell unrelated products and services, unless a request is initiated by the participant.

The crux of the issue revolves around whether participant data is a plan asset that could be used by a service provider with access to participant information and give rise to compensation-related conflicts of interest, resulting in prohibited transactions. The issue of plan and participant data remains unsettled from a legal perspective, but it's clearly an area that plan sponsors and fiduciaries will want to stay abreast of. It's likely that similar claims will be a future battleground for plaintiffs and defendants. At a minimum, I expect that contracts will evolve to address specific concerns associated with data, technology, and privacy issues.

CYBERSECURITY

The increasing usage and reliance on technology comes at an additional cost—security. A recently filed ERISA lawsuit underscores the importance that cybersecurity plays in the fiduciary process, both for plan sponsors and service providers, and could serve as a harbinger of things to come.[64] In April 2020, a complaint was filed in Illinois, naming Abbott Laboratories (the plan sponsor) and Alight Solutions (the recordkeeper), alleging fiduciary breaches of duty for cyber fraud.

In December 2018, a retired former employee of Abbott Laboratories alleged that an unknown individual accessed her account and stole $245,000 due to insufficient security measures. According to the complaint, there was no security question routine that was enforced on the benefits website. The unknown user accessed the plaintiff's account via the internet, chose the "Forgot Password" option, entered the last four digits of the plaintiff's social security number and her date of birth, and then elected to receive a one-time code via email to her email account instead of answering online security questions. The unknown user then entered the one-time code, accessed the account, changed the password, and added direct deposit information to a third-party bank account.

Here's where the story gets even more interesting. According to the lawsuit, "Two days later, on December 31, 2018, an unknown individual (the 'Impersonator') contacted the Abbott Benefits Service Center, claiming to be [plaintiff]," the complaint states.

> The Impersonator called from the phone number…which did not belong to [plaintiff], had never been used by [plaintiff] and was not associated with [plaintiff's] plan account. The Impersonator told the customer service representative that they had tried to process a distribution online, but were unsuccessful. Defendants' customer service representative, in a gross dereliction of duty, asked the Impersonator if they still lived at [the plaintiff's address], thereby providing personal information to the Impersonator.

Further, the plaintiff was notified nearly ten days later via mail that the $245,000 had been transferred. However, according to the complaint, the plaintiff had elected to receive communications electronically as her preferred method, rather than via mail, and alleged that if she had been sent an email, she could have responded quickly and halted the transfer.

The complaint specifically alleges that the defendants breached their fiduciary duties of loyalty and prudence

> by causing, allowing or processing unauthorized distributions of [plaintiff's] account assets; failing to confirm authorizations for distributions with [plaintiff] before making distributions; failing to provide timely notice of distributions to [plaintiff] by telephone or email; failing to identify and halt suspicious distribution requests, such as requests for multiple distributions to accounts in different banks; failing to establish distribution processes to safeguard the plan's assets against unauthorized withdrawals; failing to monitor

other fiduciaries' distribution processes, protocols and activities; and related acts and omissions.

Now it remains to be seen whether this lawsuit has any merit, but it's unlikely to be the last of its kind. And this isn't simply an Abbott Laboratories or Alight Solutions issue, especially with so much of our financial lives moving to the digital world. This is an issue that impacts every single recordkeeper (or other vendor) in the industry that has personally identifiable information (PII) and, by extension, the fiduciaries that select these vendors. From a user experience, policies like security questions and answers, complex passwords, two-factor authentication, timed log-off, strong encryption, secure email, and voice recognition technology will become table stakes if they haven't already. From a security infrastructure perspective, recordkeepers will need to continue to invest in and deploy customer verification measures, systems surveillance, and fraud detection, stronger firewalls, and restricted user access to data. One recordkeeper even invested $50 million in a security software company![65]

Lawmakers and regulators are also starting to focus on cyber issues. For instance, in 2019, two senators wrote the comptroller general of the US Government Accountability Office (GAO) asking him to examine the cybersecurity of the private retirement system.[66] In particular, the letter identified retirement accounts as

a tempting target for criminals who could hack into a plan and individuals' accounts to access information, commit identity fraud, and steal retirement savers' nest eggs. It is important that workers and retirees know their savings are in fact safe, and that a cyberattack will not throw the retirement they have spent years working and planning for into jeopardy.[67]

That certainly sounds a lot like the Abbott Laboratories complaint.

The Advisory Council on Employee Welfare and Pension Benefit Plans, generally referred to as the ERISA Advisory Council, was established under Section 512 of ERISA to advise the secretary of labor on matters related to welfare and pension benefit plans. In 2016, it published a report examining cybersecurity considerations as they relate to pension and welfare benefit plans. While the report does not represent the position of the DOL, it does offer a number of important insights for fiduciaries to consider. John Hancock culled these six helpful cybersecurity best practices from the report:[68]

1. Prudently select and monitor third-party service providers with a process that includes investigating how PII is protected, and document the factors taken into consideration. Request information regarding the providers' data security systems and policies. Also, review the results of providers' SOC 2 audits and other industry-recognized certifications.
2. Review and, if necessary, amend agreements with service providers to ensure that contractual provisions mandate the protection of plan data and the allocation of liability.
3. Consider buying cyber-liability insurance or include cyber provisions in existing liability policies. Policies should cover liability resulting in litigation, as well as the cost of and assistance and resources (such as credit monitoring or technical support) needed to minimize the impact of an actual breach.
4. Document, review, and update cybersecurity policies for comprehensiveness. Ensure the ongoing monitoring of any covered service providers and employees with access to plan data while also limiting the amount of data available to only what's necessary.
5. Continue to educate fiduciaries (retaining an expert's assis-

tance, if necessary) to ensure they're informed regarding the functionality of the systems, as well as the processes and procedures involved with the maintenance, retention, and protection of PII.

6. Educate participants to do their part to protect against cyber-security issues before they occur—and communicate how to mitigate losses if information is compromised.

7. ERISA fiduciaries should ask cybersecurity-related questions as part of the vendor RFP process, or as a stand-alone request, and make sure this due diligence process is documented. For a list of cybersecurity questions you should ask, please visit FiduciaryU.com.

Conclusion

One of my favorite people in history is Teddy Roosevelt. Our twenty-sixth president, Roosevelt was a statesman, politician, conservationist, naturalist, and writer. But in all these things, he was a man of action. One of my favorite T.R. quotes is "Knowing what's right doesn't mean much unless you do what's right."

As a fiduciary, you have the power to change the course of people's lives (and future generations) through the choices you make. Don't settle for mediocrity or even failure. Leadership requires you to live up to a higher calling and the courage to make hard decisions for others that you know are right.

I hope the concepts, ideas, and information in this book have made you a smarter, more knowledgeable ERISA fiduciary because knowing is half the battle. Taking action with the other half is up to you.

Acknowledgments

I have to start by thanking my awesome wife, Jessica. From being my cheerleader, to helping me brainstorm concepts and ideas, to holding down the fort at home during long periods when I sneaked off to write. Thank you so much, my love. I also want to thank my four amazing kids—Caleb, Lydia, Philip, and Eli. I love each one of you more than you can imagine, and I am so proud of the young people you're becoming. I pray that I can be the father you need and deserve.

I want to thank my partners at Greenspring Advisors—Pat Collins, Matt Cellini, Greg Hobson, Jeff Bernfeld, Bob Bogue, Greg Plechner, and Molly Goetz—for their support of this project. To the other members of our Institutional Team—Lauren Gwinn, Christian Stanley, Reiley Crosby, Molly Burton, Zack Hubbard, and Khaalid Kamara—working with each of you every day is a blessing, and I am constantly blown away by your passion and dedication to the success of our clients and their participants. I am proud of each of you. And I also want to acknowledge the rest of my friends and colleagues at Greenspring who add so much to our culture and the work we do to improve the lives of the people we serve. Thanks for making Greenspring such a great place to work.

And to the many clients I've had the privilege to work with over the years: thank you for trusting our team, following our advice, and partnering with us in the fiduciary process to improve the lives of your employees and their families.

To the many industry colleagues who contributed to the success of this book, including Fred Reish, Todd Lacey, Ann Schleck, David Booth, Daniel Essman, Marcus Schafer, Fielding Miller, Rick Shoff, Greg Long, and Matthew Wolniewicz—thank you for offering me your friendship, encouragement, wisdom, and support over the years.

A big thank you to my editor Greg Brown at Yellow Barn Creative for helping shape and clarify my thoughts and words. You made me sound far better than I could on my own.

Also, to the publishing team at Scribe, including Maggie Rains, Zach Obront, Rachael Brandenburg, Tiffany Fletcher, and Rikki Jump. Thank you for helping bring this book to life.

And finally, and most importantly, I thank God—Father, Son, and Holy Spirit—for blessing my life in more ways than I could ever possibly imagine or deserve.

About the Author

JOSH ITZOE is a co-founder, partner, and chief strategy officer at Greenspring Advisors, a registered investment adviser (RIA) and the 2018 PLANSPONSOR Retirement Plan Adviser of the Year—Small Team. He is also the host of the Fiduciary U Podcast and creator of FeeMetri(k)s.

Recognized as an industry expert and thought leader in the world of defined contribution plans, he specializes in fiduciary oversight, investment due diligence, fee benchmarking, plan design, and vendor management. He is a CERTIFIED FINANCIAL PLANNER™ professional and Accredited Investment Fiduciary®.

A passionate advocate for fiduciary principles, *The Fiduciary Formula* is Itzoe's second book on fiduciary responsibility. In 2008, he wrote *Fixing the 401(k): What Fiduciaries Must Know (and Do) to Help Employees Retire Successfully*.

A frequent industry speaker, Itzoe has also been quoted extensively in publications such as the *Wall Street Journal*, *SmartMoney* magazine, *Kiplinger's Retirement Report*, *InvestmentNews*, *PLANADVISER*, and *PLANSPONSOR*.

Prior to Greenspring Advisors, Itzoe started his career in financial services at Morgan Stanley and also played professional baseball for several years after college. He lives outside of Baltimore with his wife and four kids.

To learn more about Josh and his work, please visit Greenspring Advisors.com, FiduciaryU.com, and FeeMetriks.com.

Notes

1 "Fact Sheet," US Department of Labor, Employee Benefits Security Administration, https://
www.dol.gov/sites/dolgov/files/EBSA/about-ebsa/our-activities/resource-center/fact-sheets/
ebsa-monetary-results.pdf

2 https://www.cancer.org/cancer/ovarian-cancer/about/key-statistics.html

3 https://cancerstatisticscenter.cancer.org/?_
ga=2.168822433.1800856465.1578597061-1334753481.1578597061#!/cancer-site/
Ovary

4 https://www.ebri.org/content/the-2017-retirement-confidence-survey-many-workers-lack-
retirement-confidence-and-feel-stressed-about-retirement-preparations-3426

5 ERISA Section 404(a)(1)(A)

6 *How Much Should I Save for Retirement*, Marlena Lee and Massi De Santis, Dimensional Fund
Advisors, June 2013.

7 "2019 DC Survey: Plan Benchmarking," *PLANSPONSOR*, November 13, 2019, https://www.
plansponsor.com/research/2019-dc-survey-plan-benchmarking/

8 *Building Financial Futures, 3rd quarter—2019*, Fidelity Investments, accessed January 2020,
https://institutional.fidelity.com/app/literature/item/9892751.html

9 *How America Saves 2019*, Vanguard, June 2019, https://institutional.vanguard.com/iam/pdf/
HAS2019.pdf

10 "2019 DC Survey: Plan Benchmarking," *PLANSPONSOR*.

11 *Reference Point*, T. Rowe Price, 2019, https://www.troweprice.com/content/dam/retirement-
plan-services/pdfs/secure-only/Reference-Point-Annual-Report-2019.pdf

12 "Seeking (k)larity: A Comprehensive Look at Employee Financial Wellness & Well-Being," Greenspring Advisors, 2019, www.greenspringadvisors.com/seekingklarity

13 *Reference Point*, T. Rowe Price.

14 "2019 DC Survey: Plan Benchmarking," *PLANSPONSOR*.

15 *The Impact of Auto-Enrollment and Automatic Contribution Escalation on Retirement Income Adequacy*, EBRI/DCIIA study, October 2010, accessed January 2020, https://www.ebri.org/docs/default-source/ebri-press-release/pr26e94f9d443d6688bc58ff0000a8d73a.pdf?sfvrsn=9ad4292f_0

16 Holt, Carlson, and Dey, *Morningstar's 2019, Target-Date Fund Landscape*, 2019.

17 https://www.investmentnews.com/article/20180212/FREE/180219994/target-date-assets-continue-to-climb

18 Quick Questions/Investment Mix microsite launched 8/6/13 to 3,120 targeted Fidelity Workplace Investing participant population; data as of 9/9/13. Participants were asked simple questions to determine their level of engagement or skill with regard to managing their workplace savings. Participant answers to these questions helped categorize them in two buckets: participants who manage their money on their own (23%) and participants who would like help managing their money (77%).

19 Fidelity analysis of 21,000 corporate DC plans (including advisor-sold DC) and 13 million participants as of 3/31/2014. "Not engaged" defined as those participants who have not made an exchange, changed how their contributions are directed, or used any form of guidance in the last two years.

20 *Outcomes of Participant Investment Strategies 1997–2006*, a study conducted by Burgess & Associates for John Hancock USA examining the performance of portfolios of 14,485 (ten-year) and 200,467 (five-year) retirement plan participants contributing to their employer's defined contribution plans through an ARA group annuity contract issued by John Hancock USA.

21 *Reenrollment: One year later*, Vanguard, March 2017.

22 J. I. Shaw, J. E. Bergen, C. A. Brown, and M. E. Gallagher, "Centrality Preferences in Choices among Similar Options," *Journal of General Psychology* 127, no. 2 (2000): 157–164.

23 "A Lone Range of the 401(k)'s," *The New York Times*, March 29, 2014, https://www.nytimes.com/2014/03/30/business/a-lone-ranger-of-the-401-k-s.html

24 "Public Enemy No. 1 for 401(k) Profiteers," *InvestmentNews*, March 21, 2014, https://www.investmentnews.com/article/20140126/REG/301269992/public-enemy-no-1-for-401-k-profiteers

25 John Oliver, "Retirement Plans: Last Week Tonight with John Oliver (HBO)," YouTube video, 21:29, https://www.youtube.com/watch?v=gvZSpET11ZY&feature=emb_title

26 George S. Mellman and Geoffrey T. Sanzenbacher, "401(k) Lawsuits: What Are the Causes and Consequences," Center for Retirement Research at Boston College, No. 18-8, May 2018, https://crr.bc.edu/wp-content/uploads/2018/04/IB_18-8.pdf

27 "Jerome Schlichter—Senior Partner—Schlichter Bogard and Denton," Schlichter Bogard and Denton, https://www.uselaws.com/attorneys/jerome-schlichter/

28 ERISA Section 404(a)

29 "Who Are You Calling a Fiduciary?" *Context* (blog), AllianceBernstein, February 10, 2015, https://blog.alliancebernstein.com/post/en/2015/02/who-are-you-calling-a-fiduciary

30 https://www.dol.gov/sites/dolgov/files/ebsa/about-ebsa/our-activities/resource-center/publications/understanding-retirement-plan-fees-and-expenses.pdf

31 https://www.dol.gov/sites/dolgov/files/EBSA/about-ebsa/our-activities/resource-center/publications/a-look-at-401k-plan-fees.pdf

32 Fidelity Investments Guaranteed Income Estimator, male, starting at age 65, single life immediate annuity (no increase option or death benefit), state of Maryland, 1/9/2020. $200,000 in assets would purchase $1,022 in monthly income for life.

33 Fred Reish, Chair, Financial Services ERISA Team, Drinker Biddle, *PLANSPONSOR*, August 2015.

34 Department of Labor, Field Assistance Bulletin No. 2003-03, https://www.dol.gov/agencies/ebsa/employers-and-advisers/guidance/field-assistance-bulletins/2003-03

35 According to the most recent prospectus and as listed on the American Funds website (https://www.capitalgroup.com) as of December 2019.

36 Data provided by Morningstar.

37 https://www.dol.gov/sites/dolgov/files/EBSA/about-ebsa/our-activities/resource-center/publications/a-look-at-401k-plan-fees.pdf

38 *Defined Contribution Plan Participant Survey Findings*, JPMorgan, 2016.

39 "Seeking (k)larity: A Comprehensive Look," Greenspring Advisors.

40 https://ahajournals.org/doi/abs/10.1161/01.CIR.37.4.549

41 S. S. Iyengar and E. Kamenica, *Journal of Public Economics* 94, nos. 7–8 (2010): 530–539.

42 *How America Saves 2018*, Vanguard, June 2018, https://pressroom.vanguard.com/nonindexed/HAS18_062018.pdf

43 David, Kinniry, and Sheay, "The Asset Allocation Debate: Provocative Questions, Enduring Realities," Vanguard, 2007.

44 Gary P. Brinson, L. Randolph Hood Gilbert, and L. Beebower, "Determinants of Portfolio Performance," *Financial Analysts Journal* 51, no. 1 (January 1, 1995).

45 "2019 DC Survey: Plan Benchmarking," *PLANSPONSOR*.

46 US Department of Labor, Employee Benefits Security Administration, "Target Date Funds—Tips for ERISA Plan Fiduciaries," February 2013, http://www.dol.gov/ebsa/newsroom/fsTDF.html

47 https://www.investopedia.com/terms/s/survivorshipbias.asp

48 Ecole Polytechnique Fédérale de Lausanne, "How Stress Tears Us Apart: Enzyme Attacks Synaptic Molecule, Leading to Cognitive Impairment," *ScienceDaily*, September 18, 2014, https://www.sciencedaily.com/releases/2014/09/140918091418.htm

49 Ted Godbout, "Financial Wellness Initiatives: Broad Interest, but Little Consensus," NAPA Net, December 4, 2019, https://www.napa-net.org/news-info/daily-news/financial-wellness-initiatives-broad-interest-little-consensus

50 "Seeking (k)larity: A Comprehensive Look," Greenspring Advisors.

51 Kristine Dery and Ina M. Sebastian, *Building Business Value with Employee Experience*, MIT CISR Research Briefing 17, no. 6 (2017), https://www.avanade.com/-/media/asset/thinking/mit-research.pdf. Innovation was measured by the percentage of revenues from new products and services introduced in the last two years. Customer satisfaction was measured by industry-adjusted Net Promoter Score (NPS) 2016.

52 *Most Americans Don't Have a Financial Plan, and Many Think Their Wealth Doesn't Deserve One*, Charles Schwab, May 15, 2018. https://pressroom.aboutschwab.com/press-release/schwab-investor-services-news/most-americans-dont-have-financial-plan-and-many-think-t

53 "Seeking (k)larity: A Comprehensive Look," Greenspring Advisors.

54 https://www.morningstar.com/blog/2018/03/12/fund-flows-charts.html

55 *Selecting an Auditor for Your Employee Benefit Plan*, US Department of Labor, September 2018, https://www.dol.gov/sites/dolgov/files/EBSA/about-ebsa/our-activities/resource-center/publications/selecting-an-auditor-for-your-employee-benefit-plan.pdf

56 *Assessing the Quality of Employee Benefit Audits*, US Department of Labor Employee Benefits Security Administration, May 2015, https://www.dol.gov/sites/default/files/ebsa/about-ebsa/our-activities/resourcecenter/publications/assessing-the-quality-of-employee-benefit-plan-audits-report.pdf

57 1 Peter 4:8 (New International Version).

58 https://www.shrm.org/ResourcesAndTools/hr-topics/benefits/Pages/pay-or-401k-match.aspx

59 Glassdoor Employment Confidence Survey, October 2015.

60 Kayla Tausche and Chloe Aiello, "Tax Reform Prompts Visa to Raise 401(k) Match for Employees," CNBC, January 8, 2018, https://www.cnbc.com/2018/01/08/tax-reform-prompts-visa-to-raise-401k-match-for-employees.html

61 Tausche and Aiello, "Tax Reform Prompts Visa" (emphasis mine).

62 https://rework.withgoogle.com/guides/set-goals-with-okrs/steps/understand-moonshots-vs-roofshots/

63 https://www.groom.com/wp-content/uploads/2019/04/Settlement-in-Vanderbilt-403b-Case-Raises-Plan-Data-Questions.pdf

64 https://www.pionline.com/courts/abbott-labs-alight-sued-over-401k-security-breach.

65 https://techcrunch.com/2016/01/21/security-startup-malwarebytes-raises-another-50m-from-fidelity/

66 https://www.plansponsor.com/lawmakers-ask-gao-examine-cybersecurity-retirement-system/

67 https://www.help.senate.gov/imo/media/doc/190212%20GAO%20Retirement%20Cybersecurity%20Request.pdf

68 https://retirement.johnhancock.com/us/en/viewpoints/erisa--plan-design/cybersecurity-and-your-401k-plan-fiduciary-duties

Index

A

Accredited Investment Fiduciary® (AIF®), 193
allocating fees, methods of
    per capita, 106–108, 114–117
    pro rata, 106–108, 114–117
American Institute of Certified Public Accountants (AICPA), 212, 214, 220–221
Ariely, Dan, 73, 230
artificial intelligence (AI), 230–231
asset allocation, 142–143
asset-based formula, 108
automatic features
    case study, 75–76
    implementation strategy of, 75–76

B

behavioral economics, 56, 73, 141, 229–230
behavioral finance concepts, 53, 141
Benartzi, Shlomo, 56
benchmarking, 24, 85, 102, 123, 125–126, 188, 195, 201–202, 234
Berra, Yogi, 223
Brin, Sergey, 227
Burton, Molly, 25

C

Cellini, Matt, 25
Center for Research in Security Prices (CRSP), 153
Certified Financial Planner (CFP), 193
Certified Plan Fiduciary Advisor (CPFA), 193
Certified Retirement Counselor (CRC), 193
Chartered Financial Analyst (CFA), 193
Chartered Retirement Plan Specialist (CRPS), 193
Collins, Pat, 23
committee charter, 24, 38, 47, 49–50
communities, 181, 185
confidence, 30, 54, 59, 61, 169–180
Crosby, Reiley, 25
cybersecurity, 235, 237–239

D

data privacy, 234
De Santis, Massi, 59
decision-making process, 45, 73, 131, 180
deficiencies, 212, 214, 219
Defined Contribution Institutional Investment Association (DCIIA), 67, 78
Department of Labor, US (DOL), 34, 38, 40, 45, 82, 94, 96, 108, 123, 129, 134, 145–146, 160, 165, 211–214, 219, 232, 238
Dimensional Fund Advisors (DFA), 59, 61–62, 153–154, 164
diversification, 143–144, 159–160, 227
Doerr, John, 226, 229
do-it-yourself (DIY), 68, 140, 142, 160, 163

E

Einstein, Albert, 26
employee benefit plan (EBP), 41, 210–214, 219–221
Employee Benefit Research Institute (EBRI), 54, 67, 78
employee benefits liability insurance (EBLI), 41
Employee Benefits Security Administration (EBSA), 34, 49, 212, 232
employee responses, comparison of, 177
Employee Retirement Income Security Act (ERISA), 17–19, 34, 40–41, 46–48, 55, 103, 136–137, 140, 143, 146, 192–193
employees, career stages of
    early career employees, 174
    late-career employees, 175

mid-career employees, 174
ERISA fiduciaries, 17, 239
escalation, 55, 66–67, 71–72, 75–79, 102, 174, 198, 216, 226, 233
exchange-traded funds (ETFs), 149, 202

F

fee structures within industry
  asset-based, 104
  fixed, 104
  per participant, 104
  revenue sharing, 104
  transactional, 104
fiduciaries
  advisor, 91, 191–193, 198, 201, 206
  considerations, 140–141, 161
  ecosystem, 17–18, 30
  expertise, 18, 40
  governance, 15, 27, 35, 40, 45, 102, 188, 191, 195
  insights for, 238–239
  Method, 29
  training, 24, 38–40, 44, 48–50
fiduciary ecosystem
  full-time fiduciaries, 18
  full-time fiduciary support staff, 18
  part-time fiduciaries, 18
  part-time fiduciary support staff, 18
Fiduciary Formula
  how it works, 27–28
  six elements of, 28
fiduciary training curriculum, areas of
  best practices, 40
  fiduciary liability, 39
  fiduciary status, 39
  hot topics, 40
  litigation lessons, 40
  overview of ERISA, 39
  plan fees, 40
    company, 105
    participants, 105
  plan investments, 40
  plan management, 39

vendor selection, 40
financial
    plan, 174–175, 179–180
    stress, 84, 167, 169, 171, 173–174, 177, 179, 181
    well-being, 167–171, 225
    wellness, 167–168, 170–171, 178, 182
fixed fees, 108, 119
Fixing the 401(k), 24–25, 68, 82
flexibility, 115, 117, 136, 140, 159–161
formal retirement committee, 24, 46, 49
401(k) plans, 21, 68, 88, 90, 142, 145, 194
403(b) plans, 87, 89, 91, 119, 125, 127, 139, 234
fund menu design, 139, 141

G

Generally Accepted Auditing Standards (GAAS), 211–212, 219
Gillette model, 200
Greenspring Advisors, 21, 30, 65, 72, 136, 149, 182, 184, 227
Gwinn, Lauren, 25

H

Hancock, John, 238
Health Savings Accounts (HSAs), 231
hiring decision, traits of well-informed
    business model, 192
    certification and licensing, 193
    commitment as a fiduciary, 193
    ERISA specialist, 192
    industry thought leader, 193
    innovation, 193
Hobson, Greg, 25
Hubbard, Zack, 25

I

Interpretive Bulletin (IB), 134
Investment
    Process, 15
    Theory, 159
Investment Association (DCIIA), 67, 78
Investment Policy Statement (IPS), 24, 40, 44, 47, 50, 133–137, 161–165,

188
  best practices for, 133
  tips for well-constructed, 136–137
Iyengar, Sheena S., 142

J

JPMorgan, 68–69, 139, 163

K

Kamara, Khaalid, 25
Kamenica, Emir, 142
key performance indicators (KPIs), 227
(k)larity®, 25, 30, 182

L

Lacey, Todd, 25
lawsuits with largest excessive fees
  ABB, 129
  Boeing, 129
  Lockheed Martin, 129
Lee, Marlena, 59
litigation trends, 87, 198

M

machine learning (ML), 231
Markowitz, Harry, 144
Measure What Matters, 226
meetings, 37, 43, 46, 48, 50, 178, 185, 189
monitoring, 40, 43, 88, 102, 111, 145, 157, 164, 191, 195

N

natural-language processing (NLP), 231
Nudge: Improving Decisions about Health, Wealth, and Happiness, 141

O

OKR-type approach, 227
Oliver, John, 84
open architecture, 198, 200–201

P

Page, Larry, 227
Participant
    by participant basis, 115–116
    Solutions, 230–231
    Support, 15, 28, 215
passive management, 149–150
pathways, 181, 185
payment, indirect sources of
    forfeitures, 105
    revenue sharing, 105
Pension Protection Act, 56, 145
Pink, Daniel, 56
Plan
    Auditor, 19, 209
    Design, 216, 228–229, 233, 245
    documentation, 24, 46
Plansponsor magazine, 63, 223
Predictably Irrational, 73, 230
Price, T. Rowe, 65, 67, 78, 147, 198
Provider Management, 28
public service announcements (PSAs), 81

Q

Qualified 401(k) Administrator (QKA), 193
qualified default investment alternative (QDIA), 68–69, 71, 76, 78–79, 145,
    160, 231

R

recordkeeper, 102, 200–210
reenrollment as appealing, 139
registered investment advisers (RIAs), 18, 21, 102, 192
Reish, Fred, 23, 40, 106, 136
replacement rates, 59
request for proposals (RFPs), 91, 125, 130, 196, 215, 219, 221, 239
retirement
    equation, 95
    plan, 159, 161, 168, 187–188, 191–192, 232
    specialist, 201
retirement plan, factors of
    average account balance, 103

net cash flows, 103
total assets, 103
total participants with a balance, 103
revenue sharing, 24, 40, 91, 104–105, 109–116, 124, 127, 130–131
Roosevelt, Teddy, 241

S

sandwich generation, 174
Save More Tomorrow, 56
Schlichter, Jerry, 84, 87
Schwab, Charles, 179, 184
Service Provider Partnerships, 187
service providers
    asset manager, 103
    custodian, 103
    directed trustee, 103
    recordkeeper, 102
    registered investment adviser (RIA), 102
    third-party administrator (TPA), 102
Shakespeare, William, 187
share classes, 88, 109–111, 114, 117, 130
skepticism, 188, 208
S&P Indices Versus Active (SPIVA), 151–152, 163
Stanley, Christian, 25
surveys, 38, 44, 49, 54, 70, 77, 135, 139–140, 168

T

target date fund (TDF), 40, 44, 55–56, 67–72, 78, 139–147, 160–165, 174,
    207, 220, 231
Technology Capex, 202
Thaler, Richard, 56, 141
third-party administrators (TPAs), 19, 82, 102, 109, 111, 124, 131, 136,
    188, 197–199, 203, 205–210, 214
To Sell Is Human: The Surprising Truth About Moving Others, 56
Tracey, David B., 91

X

Xponential Growth Solutions, 38, 49

Z

zero-revenue sharing funds, 116

Lightning Source UK Ltd.
Milton Keynes UK
UKHW041904270820
368951UK00001B/32/J